I Love You to Health!

Creating Your Authentic Self in Recovery From Addiction

Lisa Michele Wilson

I Love You to Health!
Creating Your Authentic Self in Recovery from Addiction

Copyright © 2015 by Lisa Michele Wilson

All rights reserved. No part of this publication may be reproduced, distributed, or transmitted in any form or by any means, including photocopying or other electronic or mechanical methods, without the prior written permission of the publisher or author, except in the case of brief quotations embodied in reviews and certain other noncommercial uses permitted by copyright law. For permission requests, email the author at lisamichele@comcast.net.

The content of this book is for general instruction only. Each person's physical, emotional, and spiritual condition is unique. The guidance in this book is not intended to replace or interrupt the reader's relationships with any healthcare professionals, a sponsor, or counselor. Please consult your physician or other healthcare professional for matters pertaining to your specific health, medications, and diet.

To contact the author or publisher, visit
lisa-michele-wilson.com

Copyright © 2015 Lisa Michele Wilson
All rights reserved.
ISBN: 0692394788
ISBN-13: 978-0692394786

Dedication

For those not yet in recovery, those who have taken that giant leap, and the family and friends who love them. And for Matthew, who makes the world a better place: To Infinity and Beyond, Beyond

Contents

Acknowledgements	vii
Introduction	ix
Chapter 1: **Rock Your Recovery**	1
Chapter 2: **The Substances**	22
Chapter 3: **Reclaiming Your Authentic Self**	27
Chapter 4: **Finding Your Healthy Balance**	40
Chapter 5: **Help is Available Every Step of the Way**	53

Chapter 6:
Nourishing Your Authentic Self 66

Chapter 7:
Relapse Ahead? Take a Detour Back to Yourself 75

Chapter 8:
**Your Dreams and Beyond:
Your Safe, Sober, and Spiritual Self** 91

Resources for Recovery 107

Selected Bibliography 113

Share Your Recovery Journey 117

About the Author 119

Acknowledgements

I AM GRATEFUL for everything in my life that has inspired me towards this writing journey. There have been special friends, family, and loved ones I have encountered over the years. Each has touched my heart in immeasurable ways. I write this for them, as well as for any others that I can reach, so that they, too, may know their innate gifts.

Introduction

I WANT TO help you find your greatness within. You do not have to develop it. You do not have to invent it. It is already there. You just have to find it! This book can help you do it. Its purpose it to give you a few easy tools and bits of information intended to guide you in that quest to find your already existent and genuine greatness. Yes, I said greatness. Part of what slips up so many people in recovery is a little voice within that can be full of self-doubt. Sometimes it whispers, and sometimes it roars that somehow something is going to go wrong. You may hear your own little committee shouting, "I am going to fail! I am not good enough! I don't have what it takes. This will go wrong no matter what I do." And when anyone starts to feel that they are not deserving enough, self-sabotage approaches.

    Seriously, we don't even know when this is happening. Maybe you can think of a time recently—a time when everything was going along smoothly and perfectly, and then something unexpected happened—some commonplace, everyday frustration to make it all crash apart. You know what I mean. Whether you are in recovery, a family member, devoted mother, father, or friend, we've all been there before. We've seen the disease of addiction wreak havoc on ourselves and the ones we hold close to our hearts. What I will suggest is that in order to combat addiction, you have to put your own inner self-doubt in its place. It is not a useful part of your life anymore.

What's important to know is that we are all in this together. You are not alone, and you never have to be. Everyone needs a guardian angel. Even I did, and I was lucky enough to find more than one. So long as I have anything to do with it, you will know that you are not alone either. I hope this it is somewhat comforting to know that there are people out there who understand. I really do understand, and I assure you that you are not on this journey by yourself. None of us really ever are. We are all spiritual beings in this material world—as that song goes.

But getting back to the topic…what are the underlying reasons for self-sabotage? Could it be that we were just unlucky to experience a long series of unfortunate events? Were we too optimistic? Were we just in the wrong place at the wrong time? Are we paying enough attention to what's going on? It never seems to make any sense, and nobody can really figure out how something that was going along all fine and well suddenly falls apart. And I mean really suddenly. How does addiction creep up on you with such cunning?

What I've seen too many people do in early recovery is unconsciously *stop* taking the small steps needed every day to simply keep moving forward. Now why would you or anyone do this?

I believe it is because we are too attached to the outcomes, the immediate results, and the instant gratification for just about everything we want for ourselves. We want to have one year of recovery, but we want it *today*. We want our friend or our child to be safe. Immediately. We don't want to have to worry anymore—ever—about the future, about relapsing, about our fears.

This isn't to say that we shouldn't have expectations for ourselves or for those we care about—that we should just live one day at a time gliding along in oblivion, and forget about anything else that might happen after the day is over.

Know that living one day at a time is absolutely essential. To focus on just the moment—particularly in early sobriety or during crisis—is critical and especially important during the first few months of sobriety. And living one day at a time can be a difficult enough task for some people at the beginning without worrying about anything else. It's the perfect place to start—no doubt.

It's definitely a great principle to live by, too. And it should be enough to know that today you did the best you could in every situation. Then simply let what is out of your control lay there (and stay there).

That said, just because we live one day at a time, does not mean that we cannot take one (or more) small step(s) each day that may be likely to carry us to where we might dream we could be on another day. Take the small step today. Take one every day. Walk forward. Then simply let go of the outcome.

I will not pretend to represent any recovery program or regurgitate Alcoholics Anonymous (AA) literature—that is definitely not my department (and this book may not be 'AA-approved'), but I can and will subscribe to the basic slogans, as we do need to "Let go and let God."

But if you don't happen to have a particular religion, don't worry about it too much. That's okay, too. If there is one major takeaway here, this is it: All you need to really do is your best and give it to the angels, your higher power, or simply your "G.O.D.—Good Orderly Direction"—nothing more, nothing less. But do your best—whether in recovery or merely a bystander of a loved one going through it.

My hope is to simply lend a hand to you along the way—so that you may realize the innate gifts you already possess—to embrace yourself (and those around you) in a loving and accepting way. This is the best gift you can give yourself. May you be blessed and find small miracles every day on your recovery journey. I'm sure you will. I personally have been inspired to take another step forward and share with you and others in early recovery. I have come full circle in my life, and the goal of this book is to help you get back to your original "perfection."

Perfection? Really? Let me explain what I mean by that. There is something behind this! You are still developing. You are a work in progress. But your happiness, your idea of what it would mean to live an incredible life is simply the basis of your original creation. It's where you started when you were born into this world. I have been sidetracked so many times along the way, as you may have been, too, by unfortunate events and circumstances. Now I am writing about getting back to your original authentic self—the one that has always existed. To put it another way, no matter where the journey started for you or for anyone else, we are all born perfect. Perfectly happy, perfectly innocent blank slates ready to experience joy and love.

Unfortunately, for so many, the events in their life involve so much pain and misfortune that they are led to pick up substances to mask the experience and do not come out on the other side in one piece. I have seen this too many times. And it has been weaved into my personal experiences with friends and loved ones over the years. I would have done anything I could of personally to prevent this if I could—to be the best person I could possibly be. And to give of my constant, firm loving-kindness whenever possible. I hate being a bystander. Still, it could not be prevented. And now it is time to pick all the pieces up.

That's where we begin. I will introduce some ways in which this is done—that is, how to wrap up the pain, beautifully packaged, with a bow on top. To show how we can all ultimately reach the other side of the rainbow—through everything we've been through and extricate ourselves from the shadows as well as the darkness that we often find ourselves in. To let people who are spiritually afflicted get in touch with themselves and realize their spiritual perfection once again—as they did when they were children. When they were innocent and naive. To love themselves as much as they have loved others. To know that they are loved.

A very special person in my life sits across the table with me now as I write this. He is working a great program of recovery, and he is beautiful. And after what we have both been through, I am so proud of him and his accomplishments. He has stumbled along the way, but I know that he *knows*, as I look into his eyes. He knows his spiritual perfection. And he longs to find his purpose, too. And I hope to inspire him if I can, as he has always inspired me. And I wish to impart this on you in any small way that I can.

Addiction is a disease, as any other chronic illness, and has destroyed the lives of people from every walk of life—addiction has no prejudice. It can attack anyone at any time. Maybe at this point, you aren't sure what your story is or even why you picked up in the first place. As you recognize that addiction is a chronic and progressive illness, you have to learn how to live with it in the right way so that you do not die. Literally, so you do not die. How is one supposed to do that for the rest of their life?

There are many paths to everlasting recovery. Learning to live in recovery can be complex, so the more tools, the better. One reason for its extreme complexity is this: All the time that someone is in active addiction, their development is actually stunted or delayed. So for example, a 25-year-old who becomes clean (and has been using for 10 years) is actually emotionally only 15 years old! The person has been emotionally absent for their adolescence. So if you're a newly sober person, how do you catch up? How do you learn to cope with the ups and downs of the adult life that you now suddenly find yourself in? How do you catch up with yourself emotionally and spiritually? How do you move forward without going back to the very same crises that brought you to addiction in the first place?

What needs to happen for you or for your loved one, your sponsee, or your client is greater awareness, self-responsibility, and self-love. Learning how to live as a person who can connect with the world is the work that comes after you are physically clean. I will work very hard to show you some possibilities—with some essential tools and also by introducing a way that begins with your own willingness to understand yourself better—to tap into the parts of yourself that are genuine. Don't ever be afraid of that.

The authentic you is beautiful. Perfect just the way you are. Ultimately, every path to continued wellness in recovery begins with you. Learning how to connect. Learning how to love yourself and others. Learning that gaining your health, joy, and, ultimately, your freedom are your responsibility. When you find your individualized authentic approach to recovery, all of this can be yours. There is always love to be found. There is always hope in addiction.

With love,

Lisa Michele

1

Rock Your Recovery

YOU HAVE TAKEN the first step by wanting not only to get clean, but also to stay clean. Recovery is a process though, and everything is learned gradually rather than all at once. Nothing can be rushed. This is not a race, but a marathon! It will last a while. Every marathon does, and anything worth having (sobriety included) takes patience and commitment. You have reached a turning point and are ready to move forward—either because you have reached a bottom in life, or perhaps you have already turned that corner and you now have a *why*—that is, your own important reason to remain in recovery.

Maybe you still have to find your why. But you know in your mind and heart that you need to be clean. Today. So now it's time to get a little bit excited. You are motivated and have taken the largest first step! After all, you wouldn't have picked up this book otherwise. You have been getting somewhere lately. My goal is to help you gain momentum, and to leave you with the clear impression that you can find your own personal greatness during recovery by setting your own intentions, some short-term goals, and taking a glimpse of your aspirations. Over time, you will gain trust and confidence in the process.

Remember to gather yourself. And have a lot of patience. Even just a little bit goes a long way. Of course, patience can be hard to develop and may not happen overnight. But it will happen gradually, step-by-step, through creation of your own recovery program. Take it just one day (or even one moment) at a time.

I have created this overview to an authentic recovery especially for you. This guide and all you do in recovery can and should be further customized to be meaningful to you. That is the entire point. Think of it as a 'take what you like, and leave the rest' approach. What this means is that no single person is exactly like another in body, mind, or experience. What is meaningful and important to you is not necessarily the same as your neighbor. What may work perfectly for you in your recovery may not work at all for the next person.

You may be thinking to yourself, "Seriously? I've heard I have to do my program a certain way or I am going to sabotage myself! I have to follow the rules." So first let's make a distinction here.

Yes, there are things that you must do and recommendations that make a lot of sense to follow. Trust your instinct. For example, don't use one day at a time. Attend suggested groups regularly, find counseling, and take basic good care of yourself. Yes, there are definitely mottos to live by and best practices that you will hear about from people who have remained in recovery for some time. There are some basic rules to try and follow as closely as possible—especially early on, but it's also good to realize that you are not a robot! You are an individual, and this is where your personal program comes in. Ultimately, it is up to you to take responsibility for your personal program of recovery. It's hard to take responsibility for your program if it isn't *your* program! Make sense?

I'd like to suggest some options to add to your individual recovery arsenal. Your arsenal is your own set of tools that you put together. Each one alone is not as helpful as the group of them together. You choose everything that works for you. You own it. I'd like to help you figure out what the best tools are for your daily use. I'd also like to help you discover what else is important to you in your life right now.

I don't want to get too far ahead, but think about this: We all have similar struggles. Though we are like each other in our humanness, we are also distinct and individual in our experiences. Some of our experiences are the same. It's always good to listen to someone who has had a similar experience as our own. It makes us feel connected. But your body, mind, and spirit are not exactly like another's. This isn't to say that we aren't all human, but know that no one path to recovery is exactly identical to another's either.

You can and will find your own individual path. This is really my goal—to help you do that. Because no matter what any particular recovery program or book tells you, you must discover the recovery process that works for you—and that *you in some way manufactured* so that it is meaningful. It is up to no one else but you. You will gain the greatest satisfaction by knowing that you did it—not alone—but in a way that was completely yours to be proud of.

Top 10 Tips Today

Once you learn about different strategies, you'll choose what works best. Do not feel forced by any individual or group who tells you it's their way or the highway. However, don't dismiss what people are saying to you either. It's usually because they care. Be thoughtful in really considering the advice that you are given. Mull it over. Try it out, and see what rings true in your mind and heart.

Above all, be completely honest with yourself. Being honest is probably the single most important thing you can work on right now. During active addiction, dishonesty can become the rule. Now it's time to become authentic, which includes getting honest with yourself first, coming face-to-face with who you are, and beginning to love that person unconditionally. Here are a few tips to get started immediately. Make your recovery yours, and make it great!

1. *Work on one small step each day.* No more, no less, until you feel comfortable. Then add on if you like.

2. *Do not overestimate your ability to control* your addiction. Keep on keeping on with what is working for you. But be sure to not get complacent or lazy about it. This is where the danger lies. When you turn your back on working your program, you can get blindsided. The signs don't usually catch your attention, so you need to be on alert. Remember that addiction is a "cunning, baffling, and

powerful" disease. It will wait patiently for your weakness to emerge and let it back in. Keep moving forward in your personal growth and be highly aware.

3. *Eliminate "toxic" people from your life*. This includes friendships and romances that are affecting you negatively. Only build new healthy relationships with positive clean people. Sometimes it's hard to know who to start with, but trust your instincts.

4. *Reach out* to friends and loved ones who you may have pushed away or who have distanced themselves from you. Do it when you feel ready. This may take time… months even. Do not rush yourself. Calmly explain your boundaries and limits. You will know when the time is right. Trust your inner voice throughout the process of reconnecting.

5. *Don't mistake your desire to be clean* for the actions necessary to create real change. Your desire to be clean is great. It's really nice. But intention is totally necessary. And taking action is what makes recovery happen. Recovery includes abstinence as the first action, but it is not just about abstinence. Start with abstinence and be open to new ideas.

6. *Keep building your support network.* It takes time, but if you keep showing up, it will work for you, too. Whether this involves aftercare programs, AA or NA, or being a part of any other supportive group, build your extended family of people who understand what you're going through.

7. *Reinvent yourself* with new interests, old interests that you used to pursue, and work on discovering your true passions. Try new things. That's the only way to find what you love. Trial and error is fine. It's fun. And it's needed. It won't happen overnight. And though it may feel risky to try new things, your openness to new experiences will pay off.

8. *Be grateful.* Every day, write down 3 things you're grateful for that day. It can be anything, from the roof over your head, to a friend, family, or the food on your plate. Make it 5 things if you can. Better yet, make it ten.

9. *Stop making excuses or blaming others.* You are the only person responsible for yourself and your destiny. Truly. It's easy to blame your parents, friends, family, people who have done you wrong, or society as a whole. Yet we are who we are in spite of the hand we have been dealt. This is also tied in to becoming completely honest with yourself.

10. *Be humble.* Always be willing to learn something new each day. You have so much to offer to others, but, let's face it; we can all use some humbling at the end of the day! There's nothing to lose in learning, and it will keep you honest with yourself.

Secret Weapons in Recovery

There are hundreds of steps to recovery and better health that you can choose to take each day. You can believe that it's all up to you (as you will hear me keep saying), and you do have some control over it. (More than you know.)

Now this may sound contradictory to the first step of the 12 steps of Alcoholics Anonymous or Narcotics Anonymous, which you may have heard is:

"Admitted we were powerless—that our lives had become unmanageable."

But here's the catch:

Just because you admit that you are powerless in your old ways, does not mean that you do not take personal responsibility for your recovery to the greatest extent possible.

Part of this book is going to go into these ideas in a little more detail. But for the time being, I want to introduce some very basic self-care tips related to your overall wellness in early recovery. They are important for everyone (whether in recovery or not)! But they are especially important for you now. Knowing a little about each of these ideas will help you with the beginnings of your own self-care. These ideas will probably be at least a little familiar to you already, but reminders never hurt.

Would you agree that during active addiction you neglected yourself? Were your good habits, healthful eating, sleep, exercise, friends, employment, your financial security, and humanity replaced with bad habits, junk food, restlessness, sleep deprivation, phony friends, poverty, unemployment, and a total lack of spirituality? That's a lot to be deprived of.

Addiction isn't just about a substance, or two, or however many more that have been put into your body. It doesn't matter so much what your drug of choice is. Addiction doesn't even necessarily have anything to do with the amount that you've used. Addiction is really about the consequences of an extreme lack of self-care, including a lack of self-understanding and all the consequences that follow. Any person without self-care will self-destruct (whether through using substances or other means) in every aspect of their life.

Therefore, as you get further into recovery, self-care may be something you will need to get more familiar with, and it may not be easy at first. It might even be something you never tried. Now is finally the time to start taking care of you. Because, as you know, I want you to love yourself as much as you have loved others. And whatever your past and whatever your problems, you are not alone in them. You deserve to have the best care possible. And that care starts with you. Once you are caring for yourself, you will see the positive consequences begin to flow.

Keep it simple as you start taking steps in your self-recovery journey. Overall, recovery means getting your body, then your mind, and then your spirit back on track. In order to do this, you can begin with nurturing your body—better eating and sleeping habits, for example. Then begin creating improvement in other areas of your life, such as exercise, meaningful friendships, discovery of the purpose of your work, or in how you spend each day.

Don't expect immediate gratification and results with all of this all at once. Or think that you can do everything today. Give it months. Then give it a year. Then reevaluate what's going on. Do expect that day-by-day you will feel a slight improvement with each small step taken. Be proud of yourself for coming this far and getting ready to rock your recovery!

To start, there are several steps that are easy to take and can really add up. When your aim is to take better care of yourself, your mood improves and life changes begin to happen. Below are some of the most basic self-care steps that you can begin making:

Drink more water
Pretty simple sounding, right? Did you know that by the time you realize you are thirsty, you may already be dehydrated? You may also already know that your body is made up of more than 70% water. And that all of your systems are in need of water for ideal functioning. The right amount for you might not be the right amount for the next person. But staying hydrated is one of the single best things you can do to take care of your body today. Why? Becoming dehydrated can actually increase your cravings for the substances you are now avoiding. And just as depriving yourself of water can increase your cravings, with enough water, you may find your cravings are reduced.

Dehydration can also lead to headaches, weakness, confusion, and depression. Throughout the course of addiction recovery, water can help the body get rid of the waste and toxins that have built up over time. Now it's time to flush them out. Water is essential for circulating nutrients throughout your body. The single easiest thing you can do to feel better in recovery today is to start carrying a water bottle wherever you go. And if you used to be a drinker of alcoholic beverages, you can take up this new habit instead.

Heal through eating right
When you are recovering from addiction your body is left affected by the toxic substances that you have been putting into it for days, week, months, or even years. Nutrition is an essential part of addiction recovery, as you replenish what has been lost and also repair what has been damaged. You can facilitate your own recovery by ensuring you get enough nutrient-rich foods, vitamins, minerals, and supplements to replenish what has been lost and gain better control of your body and mood. Yes, you can actually feel more positive in your mood through better food.

Excessive alcohol and/or drugs deplete the reserves of the body. An optimally-balanced diet can help restore your appearance, your mood, your mind, and your whole life. There is enough information on healthy eating during recovery to be covered in an entirely different book. There have been some really great guides put out there on the subject, including the most essential nutrients to replenish now, why, and how to easily get them from the food you eat each day. Please see the resources in the back of this book for more information on healthy eating during recovery.

Practice simple cooking
This may sound easier to some of you than others, and you may wonder why it's even needed. I mean, you can just take a short walk, bus ride, or drive to a store and pick up

something fast and easy. Or go get some fast food. You may think that cooking takes too much time or costs too much. Plus, if you don't really know how to cook, the food won't taste very good. It can seem like a daunting task between all the ingredients, what to do, and the clean-up involved.

Would you believe that simple cooking is relatively easy, doesn't cost very much, and saves money? Believe it or not, the food that you make yourself, from whole ingredients, is more gratifying and satisfying to your body and your spirit. For the time being, it's enough to just start with a handful of ingredients. Keep it simple.

I will not make specific dietary recommendations at this time, but I would like you to know that whatever your preference, there is a really easy way for you to prepare it, just a few clicks away.

Google it. Easy breakfast. Easy lunch. Easy dinner. Even easy dessert. Substitute whatever search words you'd like. Experiment. Get a cookbook if needed. Collect the ingredients, and give just one recipe a try. If you like it, write it down, so you can repeat it. If not, try something else.

The great thing about cooking is that there is not a 'correct' way to prepare anything. You do not have to follow exact calculations or formulas. You need a few ideas and a few simple ingredients. Recipes are for recording what worked well or for sharing with others. But secret formulas are to be made up by you. There are literally hundreds of ways to prepare the same dish, and the variety is limited only to your Google search engine (for inspiration), your imagination, and the spices you have in your cabinet.

Make a habit of nurturing yourself
We all neglect ourselves from time to time. Now it's time to STOP doing that. Commit yourself to one hour per day of 'me' time where you do something that you completely love that relaxes you and puts your mind at peace. This time for you could be anything from reading a good book, picking up an old instrument, playing a game you like, going for a walk, or listening to music. Whatever it is, do something that you love, each day, every day and improve your attention to the most important person in our life—you—at all costs!

Work on healthy relationships
Relationships with friends and family may be strained now. You will not get everything that was lost back all at once or recreate instantaneous bonds. But little by little, there are ways to start repairing broken ties with loved ones and friends. Have faith that this will happen as you work your own program of recovery and rebuild trust. Yes, the trust has to be rebuilt, and the importance of that to you will shine through.

The most important tool is honesty and open communication. Start there, being as close as possible to 100% honest with yourself first. Honest about mistakes, about where you are going, and what you need to do.

You will see that slowly but surely, through your own self-care, this will become easier, and you will earn its rewards. Be patient, give it time, and start with one small step. You cannot resolve all relationships that have been damaged overnight. Your relationships will naturally fall into place when those close to you see that you have committed yourself to new and positive lifestyle changes. When you feel challenged, understand that a lot has happened, and that change happens gradually. Trust can be rebuilt.

Get regular physical activity
Exercise provides a variety of benefits in recovery, including creation of an overall positive outlook. How does this happen? Well, for starters, it increases levels of substances, known as endorphins, in the brain that improve mood. In addition, nerve connections in the brain can be stimulated by physical activity.

This can bring about healing for a brain affected by drugs and/or alcohol. Exercise helps your brain recover from the harm that has been done to it over the course of drug use.

Exercise also improves the regularity of your sleep cycle, helps control weight, and improves your circulation, your energy level, and the ability to think, feel, and connect with yourself. It doesn't have to be difficult or extremely vigorous. You really don't need to run a 5-minute mile or even lift weights. Start with something small, like a 30-minute walk. See how you feel. If there is an activity that you really love (or that you used to really love), this would be a great time to start it up again.

Find work and a life you love
When we love what we do every day (and better yet, get paid for it) life can be much easier. Getting up and actually wanting to go somewhere *and* getting paid to do that. What a concept. Many people are not that fortunate. You

can be. As you get healthier, you will be in a better position to really explore what you have been doing to earn money—whether it was a part-time job, a career you really loved, or even if you are just getting started in the work world. Regardless of what you were doing (or maybe *not* doing), it may soon be time to re-evaluate if you should continue going down the same path, or if it is time to start searching for something that is truly rewarding to you.

Develop your spiritual self
Whatever your religion or your spiritual belief, tuning into your spiritual practice (or even creating one from scratch) can is an important part of your recovery process. Know that this is not so much about a particular chosen religion, but really more about the core of who you are.

During abuse of alcohol and drugs, a person is living in direct opposition to any spiritual practice. In other words, when a person is consumed with drug and alcohol abuse, that person is running away from reality and one's true existence, relationships, and life. Here's a description of what spiritual practice can mean:

Spiritual practice can be easy and can be developed or redeveloped. At its very core, "spiritual practice" means something very simple. Spiritual practice is nothing more than being present in the moment and being accepting of whatever that particular moment is bringing you now. Spiritual practice is experiencing life without harsh judgment towards self and others—without running away from one's difficulties and challenges.

In other words, your spiritual practice means being in touch with yourself. We are all spiritual beings in a material world no matter what religion we were born into or what religion we choose or do not choose.

Developing your spiritual practice may actually be nothing more than grasping the notion of being unconditionally accepting of where you are now and being present in the moment today. When you take small steps each day to develop your awareness of these ideas, you'll see that being in this 'awake' state can help reduce and even combat obsessions, anxiety, and cravings that lead to relapse.

• • •

Developing a plan in early recovery is key to sustaining a longer-term recovery. A very good strategy to keep busy and to also help yourself form new positive memories is to change your personal surroundings. To whatever extent possible, create a new living space for yourself.

You might not be able to pick up and move to another city or even a new home, but you can definitely rearrange your room, throw out old junk, and fill your surroundings with new items, pictures, scents, and anything that you find makes your surroundings pleasantly different than what they were before. There should be few reminders left in your space of a time when you were using. As you create your reinvented living space, visualize getting rid of the parts of your life that were not working for you.

Next, seek out a 12-step meeting near you. This is usually pretty easy. Go online to your local anonymous meeting group and try at least one meeting in the area. There is also a resource directory in the back of this book with contact information for a few of the best known anonymous fellowships. Introduce yourself as a newcomer when you go. You will almost always be warmly welcomed. Within the first week or two you can try find yourself a sponsor—that is, a person who can help guide you through the program. More information on this is covered in a later chapter.

• • •

The questions here were received by me from persons in early recovery. I collected a few to share with you, since you may have the same or similar questions. The answer for each question is a combination of my own experience and answers that I compiled from people in programs of recovery:

Question: Do I have to go to AA/NA meetings?

Answer: AA meetings give you an almost always available and free tool to get you out of rough spots and conflicts. Meetings also give you a great place to speak your mind and share confidentially with a group of people who are in the same place as you emotionally. If the people at the meetings are not in the same place as you, there is at least one person and probably many more who have been exactly where you are at some time in their lives. They understand, and meetings can be, not only very comforting, but a great way to find local support a build a network to count on. Whether you go to meetings or not is ultimately your decision. I would urge you to try a variety of different meetings, since they are all different, and see if you can find one or more that you like. You can always 'take what you like, and leave the rest.'

AA and NA are what people in a recovery program often choose for themselves in order to stay in recovery long-term. If you elect not to go to AA or NA meetings, then you can strive to do something every day that helps you in your recovery, whether it's going to church or volunteering, or helping people in any way. There are many different avenues that you could go down. The important thing is that you are doing something that is moving you towards greater self-awareness, sharing, and sober connection. AA/NA is just one of the most common ways that people in recovery stay sober.

Does it work for everyone? Well, it's been around for about 70 years. I've seen it work extremely well for some people, and I've also seen people that it probably wasn't a good match for. However, it never works for anyone right away. Attending 90 meetings in 90 days is suggested. If you can do that, and then make a decision, you are giving the whole thing a pretty fair shot for yourself. Showing up is the first step. Obviously, you can't expect to just go there and expect it to work for you. You have to decide that you want to give it a try and commit to that. If you're dedicated, it can definitely work for you, as it has worked for so many. By trying one or more meetings in different areas at different times, you increase the likelihood of finding a group that you can really connect with.

Question: *It's tough to build friendships. How do I start?*

Answer: Go to 12-step meetings. Get a home group meeting. This is the one group that you go to every week at the same time, same place. This gives a strong sense of belonging. It may take trying a few different meetings to find a group of people that you feel comfortable with. There will be people there that are either currently in a situation similar to yours (or were at some point) and will be able to relate to your circumstances.

There is a sense of belonging in meetings that cannot be easily described. It can bring you peace of mind in a truly sober environment. The more you go, the more people you will run into that you have things in common with.

Question: *When telling my story in a meeting, what do I have to share? Is there anything I shouldn't share?*

Answer: You share your experience, your strength, and your hope. You might try to stay away from "war stories" and being really graphic. Sharing at meetings is more about expressing how you felt when you were in active addiction compared to where you are now, where you draw strength from, and what helps you overcome your struggles.

It's also as important to just listen and hear others' viewpoints on these same topics. This naturally helps you, since you'll be able to relate. Sharing your own issues is both healing to you and provides different viewpoints to others in your new network. If all this seems too intimidating, don't worry. *You don't have to share anything* if you don't feel like it, but the more you get off your chest, the better you may feel.

Question: *How do I deal with being around non-sober addicts or alcoholics?*

Answer: Honestly, you shouldn't be around them. Why would you want be? If you find yourself in that kind of situation, move as far away as you can—not because they are bad people, but because that environment can hinder your own recovery. You need to engage in extreme self-care, and your recovery must come first. If you are around people who are still using, then you are asking for relapse. It's self-sabotaging, so it's best to just turn around.

Stay away from persons, places, and things that are reminders of the alcohol and drug culture. Remove their numbers from your phone list. Don't communicate with them on Facebook or any other social media. If you must be around them…for example, if you work with them, and can't avoid it, make sure you have a sponsor to discuss this with or someone else to help you deal with this very difficult situation. If it can't be managed, change it.

Question: *How do I handle constant bombardment of advertising surrounding drinking—like beer and alcohol ads?*

Answer: This one is tough. The easy answer is to look away and not be drawn into the glamour of any advertisement. Change your surroundings when possible. Change the channel. Part of the process of getting clean is also accepting that reminders and triggers are in society wherever you go. This may not be the easy answer, but a lot of recovery is retraining your mind to respond in ways that are not harmful to yourself. Though we can't always control our environment, we can usually control our reaction.

You can take small steps to stay out of the way. Some things are unavoidable or unexpected. You need to partially accept that. You can also learn to view these ads through a different lens. Get a sponsor or trusted counselor, call somebody, and talk to them about it. Opening up and sharing can be enough to let the irritation subside, since it is a temporary situation.

Question: *I feel like people are judging me as someone who is in recovery. Any advice?*

Answer: This is a natural feeling. People naturally judge other people. They also make errors all the time in their prejudices and judgment. Your opinion of yourself should never be based on others' judgment of you. Opinion is not fact. No matter who is telling you, you decide what is right. Your self-worth must come from within. You have ventured into sobriety, and many people do not understand what it means to be in recovery—that is, how difficult it is and how courageous you are for being where you are.

Part of recovery is accepting and loving your true authentic self, and much of doing that means not caring so much what others think or living a life where you are only trying to please.

Remember that you do not have to share that you are going to meetings or that you are in any recovery program with anyone who you do not feel like sharing it with. You are entitled to maintain complete anonymity, which is a big part of the program. What you say in the rooms of AA or NA is confidential. More importantly, you need to be honest and true to yourself. Other like-minded individuals will not judge you. And you will find them.

Remember this:

"Be who you are, and say what you feel. Those who mind don't matter, and those who matter don't mind."

~An anonymous piece of wisdom

2

The Substances

BEFORE GETTING INTO more of the recovery process, I'd like to quickly comment on some of the most commonly abused substances—and, in particular, how they can affect your body and your brain. This is by no means a comprehensive list, but includes some of the most widely abused drugs. You are now working towards healing a destructive process. Know that your body (given half a chance) can and will heal itself. Of course, this will only happen once abstinence from the substances has begun. Some of the most profound health impacts are listed below for each substance. What each drug does to not only your body, but your mind and spirit is profound, and highly specific to each person.

Alcohol
Perhaps the most widely abused drug, people underestimate the power of alcohol to destroy the mind and body. Alcohol's immediate effects include impairment of judgment and delayed reaction time, which, of course, leads to

doing things we wish we hadn't and the potential for serious harm to self and others when behind a wheel.

Long-term effects include liver and heart disease as well as dementia and brain damage. Withdrawal from alcohol causes depression, insomnia, anxiety, hallucinations and delirium (otherwise known as "DTs").

Benzodiazepines
"Benzos" have an anti-anxiety effect, and also cause muscle weakness and confusion. Long-term use can lead to severe dependence, insomnia, anxiety, and depression. Dangerous seizures can occur if suddenly stopped after long-term abuse.

Cocaine and crack cocaine
Immediate heart rhythm abnormalities are seen with cocaine, as well as high blood pressure. With increased use, dopamine receptors in the brain are diminished, as well as a decrease in the sense of smell and other permanent issues with the nasal cavity. Diseases related to injection of crack cocaine include HIV and hepatitis B and C viruses. Withdrawal effects include pronounced craving and anxiety.

Methamphetamine
Otherwise known as meth or speed, the immediate effects include euphoria, decreased appetite, fever, insomnia, tremors, paranoia, and aggression, damage to the vessels of the brain, and increased heart rate and blood pressure. Long-term effects include psychotic behaviors and hallucinations, heart disease, and stroke. Drug-injection-related

diseases, such as HIV and hepatitis B and C viruses are a threat, as well as withdrawal issues ranging from extreme cravings to debilitating paranoia.

Amphetamines
This category includes everything from Adderall® to diet pills, with immediate effects including anxiety, euphoria, and paranoia and long-term problems, including increases in blood pressure and mental changes. Withdrawal includes shakiness, exhaustion, and depression.

Methylphenidate
Similar to amphetamines, this drug, known by the brand name Ritalin®, can lead to dangerously high body temperature, irregular heartbeat, and withdrawal symptoms similar to amphetamines.

Prescription opiates
Highly addictive prescribed pain killers include oxycodone, Oxycontin®, Percocet®, Vicodin,® and fentanyl, among others and induce sleepiness, nausea, constipation, and dangerous respiratory depression. Their highly addictive nature coincides with withdrawal that includes muscle and bone pain, insomnia, nausea and vomiting, and involuntary leg movements. Once the binding of the opiate in the brain's receptors has dissipated, the body and brain yearn for more (not to feel high, but simply to feel normal). This is not a sustainable state.

Heroin
Severe central nervous system/respiratory depression are accompanied by euphoria with the use of heroin.

Long-term injection drug use leads to collapsed veins, infection of blood vessels and heart valves, abscesses of the liver and kidney, and lung disease. Shared needle use is commonly associated with HIV and hepatitis B and C transmission. Withdrawal can be extreme and, as with other opiates, includes muscle and bone pain, insomnia, nausea and vomiting, and involuntary leg movements, along with an overall ill feeling and cold flashes.

LSD
Using LSD, otherwise known as lysergic acid diethylamide, creates a high body temperature and a range or strong emotions that are completely unpredictable. The drug causes delusions of all the senses. Unfortunately, long-term effects of even infrequent LSD use can lead to flash-backs and severe mental illness, including depression or schizophrenia.

MDMA
Also known as ecstasy or X, this drug causes a delusional sense of well-being, high blood pressure and body temperature, dehydration, and confusion. Long-term use can lead to severe alteration of the function of the serotonin and dopamine pathways in the brain. Withdrawal often results in profound anxiety and depression.

Ketamine hydrochloride
Referred to as Special K, vitamin K, and other names, ketamine can cause respiratory depression and cardiac arrest/death. Frequent or long-term use leads to depression and memory loss.

Marijuana
Also known as pot, weed, grass, herb, reefer, and a variety of other names, marijuana usually causes memory and learning problems, as well as distorted perceptions of the senses. Longer-term effects can include lung problems, psychological cravings, irritability, anxiety, and insomnia.

This is but a glimpse of some of the serious effects of the most commonly abused drugs. Now it's time to move on to your recovery and reclaim your health.

3

Reclaiming Your Authentic Self

FOR A MOMENT, I'd like you to consider what the notion of your true "Authentic Self" might mean. Everyone might have a slightly different idea of what being authentic means or who the true authentic self really is residing within the confines of the body and spirit. Hopefully, a few positive images from childhood come to mind, or maybe you can think of another time in your life when you felt happy for no particular reason at all—a time in your life when you experienced peace, joy, freedom, and contentment simply to be alive—a time when you were happy just being yourself. This may have been a long time ago.

It's possible you were focusing on your authentic gifts and talents. Everybody has at least one. Maybe you were with a good friend. You could have been by yourself outside on a beautiful sunny day, by a beach, or on a vacation. The list goes on. But whatever thoughts come to mind when you try to imagine who your true authentic self is, remember that he or she is the person deep within you who is confident, completely present in the moment, powerful, and free.

Your authentic self owns the thoughts and feelings that originate within your heart and your authentic self is not afraid to communicate ideas and experiences openly. Your authentic self stems from your heart, digests clearly in your mind, and emerges to the world spontaneously.

As you read the above, you might feel that this rings true for you, even if only in some small way. In recent moments of recovery, you may have begun to try and get back in touch with the experiences and feelings that tie into your most authentic sense of self.

Maybe you have tried to reconnect with friends or family or have recently revisited and revealed your true feelings to a trusted person, therapist, or even to yourself in a journal. It is likely that, as you progress through your recovery, these moments of authenticity will clarify within your heart and continue to be awakened. That's the beauty of recovery.

It's also possible that, as you read the above, you realize that your authentic self may be buried beneath a bunch of rubble—that you know in your heart that you have lost a piece of who you truly are along the way. And you may yearn to be the best possible version of yourself that you can be. How could you have lost your true self? You can try to figure that out. But, more importantly, how will you reclaim yourself? After all, the past is in the past. Now it's time to slowly rebuild.

Alcohol and/or drugs literally steal your authentic self. I'm sure you've heard it before and know it on some level. By virtue of putting that substance into your body and altering your mind, mood, body, and spirit, you are essentially saying farewell to your beautiful authentic self. You are accepting that you are no longer valuable, needed, loved, functional, worthwhile, or useful, as you indulge in substances to rid yourself of pain, anxiety, anger, worry, confusion, and unhappiness.

But at the same time that you temporarily rid yourself of pain, you also rid yourself of your potential future happiness. In recovery, you have removed the substances. You are abstinent. Yet because you have deprived yourself of your true authentic self for weeks, months, or years, it can feel really awkward to be clean in the beginning. At the least, there is no substance there to obliterate the pain. But there also may be emptiness – a void – that feels dark and terrifying.

Realize that the substance banished YOU. That is pretty frightening. So take away the substance, and what do you have left? At first (and it is important to remember that 'at first' literally means *only in the beginning*), you may feel this intense emptiness. Though you still have a body (albeit a rather unhealthy one) you have created a mind that doesn't feel comfortable with the skin it's in. Why? Well, in many ways it's because you haven't actually been in your own skin for any extended period!

Anything that is unfamiliar feels awkward and unnatural. Additionally, drugs and alcohol cause deficiencies in the brain (but, thankfully, reversible ones) that can make you feel depressed and out of control.

So let's go back to how you were as a child, or even earlier—to who you were when you were born. You might think, "Who cares? I don't remember that anyway." Even if you don't remember, you came into this world spiritually free, clean, and completely your authentic self, ready to take on whatever experiences were thrown your way. You were drawn to love, as all infants are. You were a pure spirit and a blank slate—meaning you had no judgment about the world. You were ready to have happiness and love impressed upon you, and you deserved that. You still do.

You were born with the energy and wisdom of the human spirit but with no prior experiences to tarnish it. Beautiful and flawless. As I mentioned before, my goal is to help you see that your perfect spirit exists within you the same as it did the day you were born. You must simply uncover, re-reveal, and accept your Authentic Self. You may recognize a few people every now and then who are clearly genuine and reveal their true authentic self each day. Perhaps you desire to be like them? You know the kind of person I mean—the type of person who inspires others and seems to sparkle with their enthusiasm and life energy. "How do they have that energy?" you may wonder.

• • •

You have no doubt experienced numerous painful events in your life that have made it very difficult to remain your authentic self. This is a defense mechanism which happens to all of us—whether we drink and/or drug or not. We become inhibited over time. We become afraid to say what we really feel. We become less creative and feel less powerful in our environments.

Maybe you were not encouraged to be authentic. Maybe you were even punished for doing so. There could have been abuse. You may have even become totally numb. When this happens, the true spirit is weakened, and you may begin to undermine your entitlement to freedom that is your birthright.

What is important is that you understand that this has happened—that you recognize and accept that you have been living in a fictional world. And also that part of the void or hole in your heart is because you aren't being true to yourself now.

Instead of relying on reliable signals to guide your decisions and actions, you are trying to fill a void. Take away the drugs, and sometimes this void becomes another person. Sometimes it becomes another addiction. But without understanding that it has happened, there is no easy solution.

If you understand and accept how you have lost this part of yourself, then you can begin to reclaim your Authentic Self.

Part of this will happen naturally through the extreme self-care measures that are part of a strong recovery program. This book is another tool in your arsenal. But what you must promise yourself is that you will not just go through the motions of taking excellent care of yourself, but that you realize that you are doing them with the *goal of continually revealing your true Authentic Self.* You are the only one who can gauge where you are in this process.

• • •

Authenticity is one of my favorite topics. I know that with practice and applying some easy principles, you can get back to your true Authentic Self. By simply beginning to recognize your innate gifts and virtues, you can journey towards authenticity. When you are real, you become a reliable person. You can experience true friendships and dependable relationships. You can accurately see where you came from and learn from it.

To start, think about what you love about yourself, the people that you love, and the things in your life (past or present) that you are passionate about. This might be an activity that you did in childhood or an interest that you haven't thought much about recently. If you do not feel particularly passionate now, then you can begin this with simply imagining what brings you energy and joy—no matter what it is. Write these things down. Then think about them while relaxing deeply. Next, think about the person that you just wrote about—after all, that person is your Authentic Self. That's how easy this first step is.

Importantly, you must stay away from negativity—whether in others or in your own self-doubt as you are developing. You are beginning to make positive changes. If there is anyone in your life who is not supportive of these positive changes, guess what? That person should no longer be an influence in your life. Being your Authentic Self is much more important than creating a false image to anyone. This is how you will get healthy. This is how you will continue in your recovery.

Next, you must stop comparing yourself to others around you. This one is tricky, but it really can be done with practice. We are bombarded daily with messages in the media, at work, while out shopping, in school, while talking to those we are close to about the way we should look, the way we should live our lives, what our future should be, and even how we should feel!

People have a lot of opinions, and it can all be really confusing. One thing I do not want to do is confuse you with my opinions. I want you to discover your own. I want you to "take what you like, and leave the rest." I put the quotes around this because I have heard it before in meetings everywhere, and there is a lot of truth to it. I'll explain what I mean.

Just because a friend, a counselor, or person at the same meeting as you has a strong opinion doesn't mean that you have to accept it or reject it entirely. It is completely up to you to align your passions with your mind and to figure out what steps feel honest to you—whatever it is you are trying to figure out.

Once you are honest with yourself, you can begin to accept yourself with unconditional love. It sounds difficult, but it's really that simple. So for example, let's say that Bob has one year of sobriety, and at an NA meeting he shares that he doesn't feel that he would really be "clean" if he was using supportive medications to avoid withdrawal (such as Suboxone®). He may have also had other negative opinions that were shared. Let's say that you are at that meeting and that you have been prescribed and are using Suboxone. That doesn't mean that you can't respect Bob's opinion, yet also have your own thoughts on it.

You can take what you like—Bob's one year anniversary, his friendship, etc., and you can "leave the rest." In other words, opinions are not fact. They are simply opinion. What is one person's opinion is not everyone's. Your honest opinion about your own recovery is what will work for you.

Carry this through to all that you absorb in life. Take what you like—that is, what makes sense to you. And leave the rest. There are no rigid rules in sobriety or in life in general. There are guidelines that are known to work in many cases, and you can try them on. The rest of it is up to you to create. Every recovery is unique to the person. Your life and experiences may be like others' in many ways. Find that common ground, and learn from it, but also respect differences. In as many ways as we are similar, we are also different, so your program can be created especially with you in mind.

Lastly, realize and accept your mistakes. If you are open to that, it's just easier to be honest with yourself. Forgive yourself for any and all of them. Others will forgive you, too, in time. For now, forgive yourself. Completely. Embrace the present moment. Explore your own ideas. And finally, let go. Let go of the past. It is over. You are no longer in the same depth of trouble you were in. The pain of yesterday has left scars and a lot of clean up to do, but it is over. Let go of other's expectations of you for today. Just be in the moment right now. Let go of yesterday's obsessions. Let go about worrying about tomorrow. Just be you. Showing up today. You are now doing the most courageous thing you can. You are being yourself.

It sounds ridiculously simple, but not as many people can honestly say they function this way. You really can. The remainder of the book focuses on more ways to enhance your ability to move closer towards your Authentic Self.

Show up; do something each day to move forward, one small step at a time. You will encounter challenges along the way. We all do. But challenges that you end up solving will help you to become clearer about who you are so that you can be joyfully here in the moment.

• • •

As you consider your Authentic Self, and what it means to be the best possible version of yourself that you can be, I also want you to consider what your "Wild Card" in life is.

What do I mean by Wild Card? Well, in poker, people often denote a particular card—say deuces, for example, as their Wild Card. This is, of course, the special card that can be anything that you want it to be to make your hand stronger. And, like poker, everyone has a hand they are given in life which, though random to some degree includes at least one naturally given Wild Card.

The Wild Card, like the deuces in poker, represents your special talent, your passion, your virtue, or whatever it is in your life that comes naturally to you and that you feel very comfortable doing, working with, and experiencing. This Wild Card, which was given as part of your inherited hand in life, is an enormous part of your Authentic Self. It is quite possible that you haven't quite discovered what your Wild Card is yet. Or maybe you haven't quite figured out how to make the most of what you know it is. But trust me, you have one. Everyone does.

When I say Wild Card, what I really mean is that, within your deck of cards (or the hand that you have been dealt in life), you will always have a positive quality that is unique to you, that you can choose to *play in any constructive way that you choose, in order to fulfill your dreams, passions, and aspirations.*

Our Authentic Selves are tapped into what our Wild Card is. Conversely, if you are not tapped into your Authentic Self, you may not be using your Wild Card to your full advantage, and you are working much harder than you have to at doing something that is either completely unnatural to you, or that you just don't particularly enjoy.

If any of these things are happening, then you aren't making the most of your naturally occurring Wild Card. The Wild Card is the freebie that you were given in life. It could be a trait that you were born with and that was both nurtured and developed early on. It could also be a strength of any type or talent that you simply have a strong passion for. You may even have more than one Wild Card. And if you do have more than one, you will likely have one that is stronger than the other.

Now if you were playing a game of cards—poker for example—and you had a Wild Card, and then didn't use it, what do you think would happen? You wouldn't necessarily lose the game. *But* you would definitely be giving up a free advantage. Who would do that?

Just keep in mind that we all have a Wild Card, which is a natural advantage in life and that is part of what makes you an individual. It may be your naturally occurring skill or even a personality trait that is just a simple part of the true and unique you. In poker, you would *absolutely* use the Wild Card if you had a bad hand. And you would *probably* use the Wild Card to improve most any hand you were given. So my suggestion is first, to discover what your Wild Card is (if you don't already have an idea) and second, to use it!

Let's put this into more concrete terms now. I'll give you a couple of my own examples. I happen to love kids. I have a natural ability to deal with all of their antics and feel really comfortable interacting with them on a level that they are comfortable with, too. When I'm with kids, I feel relaxed, and I communicate with them in a way that feels easy, fun, and also comes pretty naturally to me. For this reason, I had considered working with kids. I did not get to use my Wild Card in the way I thought I might for many reasons. I hadn't really taken a look at myself and tried to figure out what my natural gifts were. I probably didn't even think I had any. Looking back though, I can say that it was really because I didn't realize it was my Wild Card until too late in the game.

But, I did have a child of my own, and, to this day, being a parent is probably the single most fulfilling thing that I feel I have ever done.

Here's another example of a Wild Card, which is more about a trait. I like to write. It's not that difficult for me, and I have had a lot of luck communicating through my writing. It's gotten me out of many difficult situations. So if I ever find myself in a difficult situation, I can always write a letter that will be meaningful and somehow solve a problem. Knowing that I can write, and identifying it as a Wild Card, strengthens my hand in life. How? If I have a disagreement with someone or some organization, I can write a letter. If

I am late on a bill, I can send an email explanation. If I feel tongue-tied in person, I can send a note instead to work it out.

So what is your Wild Card? What is your skill, natural gift, passion, ability, or the thing that simply comes very easy to you? This trait, quality, skill, or talent is part of your natural makeup. And remember, you may have more than one Wild Card. You probably can begin to answer the question already. If you do not have any idea, ask yourself a few questions. What have you done in your life that was pretty easy and also enjoyable? Has anyone ever told you that you were really good at something? What situations have you been in where you felt totally at ease? What are your natural personality traits? Think about these questions and put some thought into discovering your Wild Card. Keep this idea in mind as you progress through recovery and weave it into your Authentic Self. It is part of you, and you will find as you continue in recovery, that becoming the best version of your true Authentic Self that is where it's all at.

Your special skill, talent, or trait is unique and effortless to you and is an important part of your Authentic Self. Do not overlook it for too long. What's equally important is that, once you find it, you come to realize just how valuable it is.

Maybe you never thought that something that you did so naturally or so well could really be worth very much. Maybe you never thought that some of your personality traits could be useful. I believe you may be greatly undervaluing yourself. This happens a lot during addiction and in recovery. You have to begin to give yourself credit now. And remember, if you decide not to appreciate and use your Wild Card, you may be missing out on the success that using it could bring you. Once you figure out what your Wild Card is, let it start working for you.

4

Finding Your Healthy Balance

THE CAUSE OF addiction may be, at least in part, a constant craving for happiness and pleasure. It makes sense. After all, who does not want to be happy? Some people have a lower threshold for pain than others, and some people have just experienced an extraordinary amount of pain and have lost their tolerance to it.

We are constantly struggling with pain and loss—loss of a friend, a family member, a pet, a job, a change in circumstances that felt secure to us. When you feel threatened by loss you may try to escape it or get away from the uncomfortable feelings associated with that loss. That is part of an instinctual survival nature, and it is a very natural part of being human.

I believe that addiction is simply an extreme manifestation of what it means to be human—that is to have excessively strong emotions and feelings. I believe that you may have succumbed to addiction because you are extraordinarily sensitive. I know that you are extremely human in that you feel so much happiness and also so much pain at times.

I have recognized these opposing qualities in some of my own experiences and closest friends. I could never understand how my friend, Carie, for example, who seemed so completely happy, could also feel such extreme pain and anxiety the very next day. It didn't make a lot of sense to me at the time. She covered up most of her pain with alcohol and anti-anxiety drugs, so that no one close to her really even knew there was a serious issue until she was deeply embedded in her addiction.

But I do realize that the addiction wouldn't have occurred in the first place if she would not have been an extremely loving, soulful, and beautiful person in the first place. I hope this makes sense. What I am trying to say is that I do not believe that addiction is any sign of weakness of personality or character. In my opinion, it is a sign of beauty and humanity. Addicts are given a bum rap. Addiction is not a moral shortcoming. In fact, it is quite the opposite.

The person with no conscience, with no consideration for the thoughts or feelings of others, is less likely to get affected and habituated to a substance than someone who is a deeply emotional and sensitive person. Put simply, a person who is less emotionally connected, less caring about others, may have less of a tendency to turn to substances to numb their pain.

Pain and negative emotions have to pass. We have to experience the pain and get through to the other side without covering it up in order to develop the coping skills and mechanisms necessary to become stronger and thrive.

Intoxication is a temporary fix to what is often a constant problem. Intoxication can't last. It's a complete delusion. Something else needs to be done to transform the problem. One day at a time, you can put one foot in front of the other. It gets easier if you do. But you have to take personal responsibility for it.

The essence of living life on life's terms as it is delivered to you day by day, is based on being conscious of your own actions. It is also based on an honest understanding of the cause and the effect that occurs with everything you choose and with every action you take.

Because you have been stuck in a habitual and reactive pattern of using, you have caused yourself more immense suffering than if you gave yourself a chance. If you give yourself a chance, you'll see that when you take positive action, there are unexpected benefits. By starting with positive steps, you can begin to eliminate patterns of addictive behaviors. Believe in yourself.

For example, by being honest with yourself and others, by acting kindly, by being generous, developing patience, and showing appreciation, you will begin to get positive reactions from the people you care about. When you do, life changes.

Negative actions, on the other hand, such as dishonesty, selfishness, stubbornness, greed, and jealousy will tend to bring negative reactions and results. This general idea comes from ancient teachings of Buddhism that suggest that all of our suffering is a result of being human in a world that is constantly unpredictable and changing.

Craving of any type (be it alcohol, drugs, food, or a person) is a natural phenomenon. It is your responsibility to understand and balance the constant state of change in your life with the acceptance of our human nature and yourself.

• • •

I want to talk about balance related to everything in the natural world, including you. One way to understand this is through the concept of "Yin" and "Yang" balance. Yin/yang originated from teachings which say that the physical world (that is what you see and experience) came out of a universal oneness. What this means simply is that everything is connected. It also means that yin/yang work together and are dependent on the other to bring balance to the whole—whether the whole world or a whole individual.

Yin and yang symbolizes how these opposite forces are at work in the world everywhere. They are complementary opposites, which means that one cannot exist in harmony without the other (Esko 11). You've definitely seen the yin/yang symbol—the white spinning around black in a circle with a white dot in the center of the black area and a black dot in the center of the white area.

Yin and yang are thought to be continuous forces that exist in *everything* in the universe, including your body, your personal experiences, your food, and your lifestyle. Any imbalance of the two opposite forces of yin and yang can bring poor health. In fact, addiction is considered to be a condition of excess yin. By beginning to recognize the imbalances in yourself when they occur and the basic forces at work, you can begin to help realign your body and mind towards maintaining a healthy balance. You can do this by starting to understand the opposite qualities of both yin and yang.

Imbalances of yin and yang can come about by strong emotions, too much food of one type or another, exposure to extreme weather conditions, over-activity, or even too much rest. Extremes of any type are thought to disrupt the delicate balance.

For example, if you become violently angry, yin becomes depleted, and yang dominates your system. If you begin to laugh uncontrollably, you are in a state where your yang is depleted and you are overly yin. This might be a good thing. But only temporarily. Too much of anything leads ultimately to imbalance and negative consequences. When someone is "grounded" their yin/yang forces are balanced.

Yin qualities might include coolness, darkness, sensitivity, nighttime, and intuitive capabilities. Likewise, yang qualities include heat, light, physical and mental strength, daytime, and logic. As you can see yin and yang are opposites. Neither is good or bad. They are just opposing forces. Awareness of this and meeting somewhere in the middle is the ultimate goal.

Yin conditions include: fatigue, burnout, depression, and mental confusion. Yang conditions include: rage and anger, headaches, stress, high blood pressure, heart disease, and general difficulty relaxing.

Just as certain environmental conditions and situations can cause excess yin or yang, food can also be mostly yin or yang. With a little bit of information about the yin or yang qualities of certain foods, you can help yourself balance your own state of yin and yang energy through dietary choices.

Very yin food choices include extra sweet foods, fruits, and raw foods. Alcohol and drugs are also considered on the extreme yin part of the spectrum. Excess of any of these can make you very happy (perhaps even too happy). This sounds like a good thing, but a good thing taken too far can be negative. Too much yin will leave you too distracted and scattered to function efficiently.

On the other hand, salty foods, cooked foods, meats, and proteins are extremely yang, and can make you feel very strong and focused. However, too much intake of foods that are too yang can also make you feel too aggressive, angry, and out of control.

These are some very basic concepts and examples of the way that food can be used to help balance your own internal state. You can start to help bring balance to your mood and your feelings by selecting foods that are neither too yin nor yang, but that are balanced. Grounding, balanced foods include whole grains, dark greens, vegetables, beans, and legumes. Many traditional rehab programs have instituted nutritional education and teach the integration of food knowledge into a total overall program of recovery.

• • •

In terms of life balance, many traditional rehab programs have also started using balancing, such as acupuncture, in treatment programs. Scientists believe that by targeting specific acupoints of the body, the yin/yang energies of the body become rebalanced. A person who is more balanced may have fewer cravings, feel more grounded, and make better decisions. There are a few different ways that scientists think this works. One theory is known as "enhancement of immunity," which simply means that by affecting the pathways of nerves, acupuncture enables the body to heal itself (Tsung-Cheng Kuo).

The "endorphin theory" is another important way of understanding acupuncture, which is really interesting when it comes to understanding its possible role in addiction treatment. It suggests that stimulating your nerve pathways increases the level of endorphins, or good-feeling natural chemicals. Endorphins are our bodies' own painkillers and make us feel good naturally. They are hundreds of times stronger than opiates, allowing the body to feel good on its own without substances.

Another popular idea is the "gate theory," which suggests that when we are out of balance, nerves get blocked. Through acupuncture, the pathways are reopened allowing healing impulses to make their way through. The feelings of pain and unhappiness then become unblocked. (Wilkinson 136)

Acupuncture, which is a balancing therapy, helps the body to detoxify itself, too, and restore blood circulation. During the detox process, the body filters out the harmful toxins that it has stored in various organs. Acupoints are associated with specific organs, allowing the body to detoxify itself without typical withdrawal symptoms (Wilkinson 136).

Drugs such as heroin and cocaine alter brain chemistry on a higher level. Evidence has shown that acupuncture may help reduce the effects of positive and negative reinforcement involved in opiate addiction (Jaung-Geng Lin 3). Combined with support programs, addictions can be balanced by a series of acupuncture treatments.

• • •

Overall, each one of us has an ideal balance that we can try to achieve in a number of different ways—whether it is through better nutrition, acupuncture, meditation and relaxation techniques, exercise, or other self-care tools. The balance that is right for you depends on your own individual body chemistry. You can maintain it by your food choices, some alternative therapies as mentioned above, stress reduction techniques, and being mindful and aware of your current feelings.

Internally, we are always striving to maintain balance between opposing forces. Some of this is out of your control. For example, the ups and downs of life are going to happen. You simply have no control over many things. We're thrown curve balls every day. It's how you deal with them that's important and helps you to avoid relapse. So even though life happens, some of the ways that you can balance your feelings and body are completely within your control, including the use of diet and learning more about the right self-care methods for you to maintain a healthy balance.

The role of Alcoholics Anonymous and other 12-step programs also help to bring balance into recovery. How does this work? Well, through working the steps of the program, it is thought that you can create a "programmed response" within yourself to avoid cravings (Ruden 91).

When you actually work each step of the 12-step program, you are creating an effective combination of "conditioned learning," along with a possible continued elevation of serotonin (or the good feeling, healing chemicals) through the process. This is just one piece of the recovery puzzle. There are many methods and outlets for creating balance related to chronic stress, addiction, and life circumstances.

With the help of 12-step programs, the craving response can be decreased. Importantly, you can begin to conquer stress on a daily basis, create greater balance in your life, and bring together the tools, treatments, and support programs that you discover work best for you.

Overall, finding your own healthy balance is crucial. When you are doing really well, you may find that you start to forget about the disease of addiction. When this happens, remember that it can come and knock you down as you become unaware or not present. So pay close attention to the principles of balance needed each day, and you will be even more likely to stay on your sober path.

• • •

Anyone can just stop drinking or stop taking drugs. Abstinence is one part of the picture, but it isn't the only part of recovery, as you'll see. Anyone can quit eating too much, stop smoking, or abstain from just about any unhealthy activity—for a period of time anyway. But whether it's for a day, a week, a month, or longer, abstinence is not what keeps you clean and sober.

Addiction damages the brain, but it also damages the spirit. You need to begin with healing your body through abstinence, of course, but also healthy lifestyle habits. At this point, you will be in a position to feel pretty good and get on with the rest of the recovery that your spirit needs. So remember that physical recovery comes first. Once your body's healing is underway, your spiritual recovery can begin.

As you continue in recovery, your spirit will evolve into something really different than it was before addiction started taking over. Working a spiritual program of recovery challenges the psyche to try things out that are unfamiliar and to create positive change in the healing brain. Your spirit can recuperate through the creation of positive relationships with others and working integrity into all your actions.

Another way to think about this is that true recovery stems from believing that you belong to something that is much bigger than yourself—that your existence is important because it is tied into something that goes beyond your mere existence alone. There is no need to necessarily think of a particular religion to believe this. Through abstinence first, you will learn that your own intoxication is merely *an illusion and postponement* of suffering to follow. While being clean, you will experience all types of emotions that were once covered up by alcohol or drugs, as well as the yearning for what you once used to cover it up. You can get through that.

Suffering is not something new. Every group of people in the world has experienced it, and every major religion in the world has addressed it.

One in particular, Buddhism, speaks specifically of the human condition and how it is related to suffering. The four noble truths of Buddhism teach that: 1) Life is suffering 2) Suffering is the result of attachment 3) Attachment is the consequence of an illusion and 4) Freedom from illusion is enlightenment.

Drugs and alcohol are common ways for people to escape the pain and fear of suffering immediately but temporarily. Addiction calls to people when they are in their weakest moments. Addiction is sneaky and devious, and finds a way to strike when you are vulnerable and seeking a way out.

Now what if you were to take suffering and turn the meaning of it upside down on your own—simply through controlling your own thought process? What if you accept that the illusion that you have created with drugs and alcohol has been merely that—an entirely temporary and completely destructive illusion?

The truth is that every person has an important purpose as a human being that can be discovered. You can always try to find the Wild Card that you were born with to help you become the greatest possible version of yourself that you can be. You may not yet know what your destiny is. That's perfectly fine. In addiction, you probably did not know or appreciate any purpose beyond yourself. Now, in your recovery, you can begin to discover just what this purpose is. If you look for it, you will find it. Recovery will always be less than complete without seeking this out. So keep your eyes wide open. The answer will probably not be immediately apparent. But through extended sobriety, you will find it.

By discovering the virtues of your own character (yes, I said virtues), you actually enable yourself to escape pain and suffering. Feelings of being trapped, resentful, afraid, scared, angry, hurt, and bitter will be replaced with feelings of gratefulness, relief, and happiness. When being high is replaced with something that helps you grow in your own self-awareness, you begin to realize that your own sobriety is truly an awakening to the greatness within you. It's always been there, and it will always be.

When you understand what your special something is, all the sacrifices and suffering can begin to make more sense. A 12-step program may be the most common way that people find something greater than themselves—including the AA or NA fellowship and giving back to that community. But it is perfectly okay to find something greater than yourself and meaningful to you in any number of ways. The 12-step programs are one common way. Yet you could be interested in a cause, an artistic passion, your family, your community, or even some aspect of the well-being of the entire human race. Seriously. Whatever your "something" becomes, a mission greater than yourself can lead you to a balanced path that makes the discovery of yourself and the meaning of life more clear (and your suffering temporary and much less).

Another way of thinking of this is the creation of your unique sense of purpose. When you start "doing your own thing," your day becomes filled with meaningful and rewarding activities. This naturally leads to a sense of renewed energy and drastically decreased interest in drugs/alcohol.

Finding your healthy balance includes seeking your core purpose. You don't need to feel pressured though. It does not have to be discovered immediately. It may take months or years. You may not be there yet, but you can find it by beginning to take small actions to balance yourself in all you do—from nutrition to exercise. When you take great care of your body first, you can then begin to think clearly. Those are the first steps. And when you think clearly, you can begin to examine what gives you a spark of enthusiasm.

If you are not fully satisfied with your job (if you have one), would you be willing to explore other possibilities and make a change? You can reflect on any ideas for your own self-development and transformation for as long as you like. You are a work in progress. We all are. Keep your eyes wide open as you go through your life every day looking at the experiences, people, and places that show up. There are often amazing opportunities right in front of you. And they may lead to the answers you've been looking for—about what your mind and spirit *really* crave, about who you are as an individual, and about the transformation to come to the best possible version of yourself that you can be.

5

Help is Available Every Step of the Way

YOU MAY HAVE already had at least a little exposure to the 12-step programs—whether it is Alcoholics Anonymous (AA), Narcotics Anonymous (NA), or related fellowships. If you haven't had any interest or have no familiarity with them, that's okay, too. They have their pros and cons. Regardless; some familiarity is a good thing.

Not everyone buys into everything that is said at every stage of recovery or in every meeting. They (meaning the greater masses at meetings) say, "It works if you work it." I know for a fact that for some people it really does. By living "one day at a time," people in recovery are able to get the help they need by simply going to a local meeting, listening to others' stories of recovery, and gaining hope through shared experiences and strategies for recovery within these safe rooms.

AA and NA fellowships offer a great (and practically free) way to connect with others who are in the same situation as you in a non-judgmental atmosphere. There are no membership requirements at all. Anyone can come anytime to any open group. Anyone can also walk out anytime, too.

What you say there stays there—meaning there is no gossip. Your story is held in strict confidence. There can be great comfort in finding this type of community just about anywhere in the world. There are meetings everywhere, and the people are all ages and generally warm and welcoming. There are a lot of positive things to be said about these programs. If you haven't gotten yourself to a meeting yet, there is absolutely nothing to lose and potentially a lot to gain by going, including ongoing sobriety, new friendship, and connecting with people who are in the same boat as you.

You might not consider yourself to be a "group" person. Let's face it; a lot of people aren't—especially during early recovery. The last thing you might want to do is go into a room full of strangers and feel awkward. Getting there may be half the battle, but the truth is that most people in the rooms have the same exact feeling and aren't generally social types—particularly without drugs or alcohol in their systems to relieve inhibition. There are no conditions for attending, so I urge you to give it a try if you haven't. The only way to get over the hesitation is to just do it. No two meetings are alike, which is part of the fun. One meeting might be a small group of people on the younger side and another might be a mixed aged group and larger. By trying a variety of meetings in your area, you can find people that you feel comfortable with. Every meeting is a little different from another, and it keeps it interesting.

Another good rule is to try making "90 meetings in 90 days." That may seem like a lot of meetings, but if you are up to that challenge, it gives you something to do in early recovery. Supposedly, the people that make it to one meeting a day for 90 days do remarkably well in staying clean. So there is nothing to lose here either. And, of course, much to gain.

All this said, a few people go and don't quite feel comfortable. One common reason is because there is talk about "giving it up" or "handing your will over" to a "higher power." That seems like a lot to ask, and it is a sticking point with some people. But it's not as drastic as it sounds. In fact, it's not drastic at all. Just remember that your higher power can be *anything* you want it to be. It is not about believing in any specific religion. Giving it up (or admitting powerlessness over alcohol or drugs) and handing your will over to a higher power simply mean trusting that *there may be* a spiritual force larger than yourself. And a way of living that can work better than what you have tried before. It's possible, right?

What you were doing was not working for you. So if you are truly not a religious person, don't worry about it. You absolutely don't need to become one now. You can simply think of your higher power as your G.O.D., which stands for your *"Good Orderly Direction."* In other words, you can go into meetings believing in nothing more than your own ability to try a new way of life that is bigger and better than the old ways you have tried so far. I guarantee they are better.

I hope that if you haven't already attended a 12-step meeting, that you give it a try. (And if you have, that you keep on going.) AA and NA have been around for years and have spread around the entire globe. Many people believe in the power of the collective group consciousness. There is a global testimony to the fact that there is something to be gained when you show up at a 12-step meeting. How much you gain is entirely up to you. You decide.

There are no laws or strict rules in the program, though there may be people who try to tell you exactly how to "work your program." They usually mean well. They want you to stay clean. It's great to find a sponsor or someone in the meetings who will guide you. There are plenty of people willing to do that, too. In fact, helping a newcomer is a piece of the process for people who have some clean time under their belts.

Ultimately, this is your recovery, and you are responsible for it. You can "take what you like, and leave the rest." I really like this saying. What it means is that if you hear just one nugget of information that you like—something that really resonates with you—remember it, and take it with you. Take it to heart, and incorporate it into your life. On the other hand, if someone talks, and you don't agree with what they are saying, that is perfectly fine, too. There will always be someone in the room that has a different opinion than you. Remember to "leave the rest." The strength of the program is through the relationships that you can form there and the one common desire that everyone has in the rooms to get and stay clean—regardless of individual opinion. There is a common goal, regardless. It's free, and for many, these programs are a central part of ongoing recovery.

Sponsorship

Sponsorship is a cornerstone of the AA and NA recovery programs—especially during the early days, weeks, and months of recovery. When you ask someone to be your sponsor, you are asking that person to be your guide in the 12-step program. A sponsor's role includes: helping the newcomer to the program understand what meetings are all about by answering questions about the 12-steps; setting up times to talk about the steps and how to implement them in your recovery; and being there during tough times when you might have the urge to drink or use.

A sponsor will make recommendations to you for handling your personal experiences during early sobriety and will confidentially listen to your thoughts and addiction-related troubles, fears, and successes. A sponsor is also a good person to have on your side and warn you when he or she feels your behavior is showing signs of relapse. As you work through the 12-steps, your sponsor is a trusted friend. Usually a sponsor has at least a couple of years of sobriety and leads a healthy drug- and drink-free lifestyle so that he or she can be a model for learning new behaviors in recovery.

You can choose a sponsor by attending a variety of different AA or NA meetings and sharing your need for a sponsor with the leader. Or you can simply approach people in meetings who you feel comfortable with and ask them to guide you. It's that easy. There is no such thing as picking a 'wrong' sponsor because the relationship can always be changed. You are not bound to any contract with the person. If it doesn't work out, you can always switch sponsors, but it's good to get someone to work with as early on in your program as you can.

Types of Treatment

In addition to traditional 12-step recovery programs, there are a variety of treatment options available to you within your budget and situation. Whatever you choose, it should be individual to you. No single treatment option, combination of options, or model works for everyone. You can try different approaches and see what feels comfortable. The reasons for this are complicated, but it is really important to realize that the field of addiction is pretty new. Though people may preach that their method, rehab, or model of recovery is the most effective, the research isn't really supportive of any one particular method or combination of treatments as being superior to another.

The easiest place to start is with the 12-step programs (described in the previous section) since they are widely available and free. There are many people that have gotten sober through this fellowship and community. That doesn't mean treatment can't or shouldn't be tried in conjunction with or instead of the 12-step fellowships.

If you are looking for additional addiction treatments, there are a large number of options for rehabilitation and outpatient treatment. Depending on what your insurance will cover, you can explore these options, too. There are literally thousands of places a person can go. There are free places, too. The Internet is a good place to start. A great website, known as "The Fix," offers reviews of centers across the country according to rankings and cost. The Fix also provides great information and resources for the recovery community.

In-patient rehab centers offer several advantages. Once you are in, you are fully immersed in the recovery process through round-the-clock programming that gets you out of the addiction mindset and environment and into a rapid plan of action. This includes quickly learning new lifestyle approaches, ways to deal with your relationships, coping skills, and self-care. In-patient rehab is a crash course in recovery, and it is really useful for people who need to be away from their current environment entirely so that they can be completely free of substances and any lurking temptations. Being in-patient also provides intensive group and personal therapy to help get to the root of the addiction as comprehensively and quickly as possible.

Out-patient treatment or I.O.P. (intensive out-patient treatment) is similar to in-patient programs in purpose, but definitely less limiting, in that these are usually programs or groups that meet a few times a week for a few hours each time—day or night. The intensive group therapy process is often enough for individuals to start a good treatment program, and can be effective for people who are not so enmeshed in their addiction that they can still function fairly well in society. Intensive out-patient treatment is also a 'step-down' approach to in-patient. That is, once you have completed any in-patient program, you can then continue your recovery in an out-patient setting as part of relapse prevention. This is actually recommended if insurance will continue your coverage in an out-patient setting.

Individual therapy is also an important part of addiction recovery and can be a piece of a total in-patient or out-patient treatment program. Through individual therapy, you can work privately to address your specific issues and situation—whether you are dealing with self-esteem, abuse, trauma, depression, cravings, or any other specific problem. Not all, but many of the counselors that can work with you in a one-on-one basis have been through recovery themselves. For this reason, they are usually excellent resources and can guide you to long-term sobriety. Addiction counselors are often very familiar with what you are going through and freely share their own struggles and hope.

Medication-assisted recovery is another option—particularly if you have struggled with opiates or heroin. With these treatment options, daily medication is taken to eliminate cravings, (cravings which can be extremely powerful). Methadone is the oldest in the class of drugs used to treat opiate dependence. Newer treatments combine the opiate, buprenorphine (an opioid partial agonist), with naloxone (an opioid antagonist), to counter the effects of the opiate. What this means is that buprenorphine interacts with the same receptors in the brain that are affected by opiates but without causing a high.

All opiate addiction causes changes in the brain that increase the number of opiate receptors, creating a need to take higher and higher drug doses to satisfy cravings. Once you have developed this increase in receptors, your normal levels of chemicals in your brain do not adequately fill the receptors with "good-feeling" chemicals. Buprenorphine sticks tightly to the extra receptors and activates them appropriately so that the brain is functioning well without causing a high feeling. And because of its "stickiness," other opiates cannot compete with it.

Treatment also contains naloxone, which is added in to prevent abuse of the medication. Naloxone fills the brain receptors but does not activate opiate receptors.

At the time of this writing, common buprenorphine/naloxone-containing brands include Suboxone® and Zubsolv®. They are a little different from each other, but both are intended to achieve elimination of the craving for street drugs and prevention of further complications that chronic abuse can cause (including H.I.V. or hepatitis B or C infection).

Another important option is naltrexone, an opioid antagonist, which has been used for both alcohol and opiate dependence treatment. Naltrexone can help heroin abusers remain abstinent by blocking the 'high' feeling associated with heroin use. Similarly, Vivitrol® is a long-acting injectable form of the same substance.

If you are interested in these types of treatments, they are available and often paid for by insurance. You may have to get a bit creative in your search for a provider, but please connect with the resources in the back of this book for assistance. You'll find listings that include free services to help people locate physicians who are qualified to prescribe these medications. You can start by going directly to the manufacturer's home pages, too, where there is usually contact information to help you get started.

I do not personally advocate for any particular treatment type, rehab, or medication-assisted treatment, as every individual and situation is different. Please speak with your healthcare provider first. With the partners you are working with in your own recovery, you can determine what is right for you. It is also a good idea to involve a close family member, if possible, as a support partner in your treatment program.

Psychiatric management is common among people in recovery who may also be struggling with co-occurring anxiety, depression, or other underlying conditions that may contribute to the desire to continue drug or alcohol abuse. You may be evaluated for underlying co-occurring disorders in treatment, and medication is something that might be considered.

With all treatment approaches, it is best to thoroughly understand the pros and cons. With any ongoing prescription medication, you will need to work at developing an open and honest relationship with your healthcare provider. By being open about your daily symptoms you can help your healthcare provider to figure out the best treatment or combination of medications for you.

In approaching recovery treatment, remember that your body and reactions to medications may be unique. Your treatment can and should be tailored to meet the specific needs, including the best combinations of support, therapy, lifestyle changes, and approaches that work for you, while addressing any co-occurring conditions and circumstances. Every person responds differently to each medication. Listen to your body; listen to your healthcare provider; and give them honest feedback on your feelings and what is and isn't working. Don't be afraid to speak up. Stay in close touch, and check in as recommended so that any medications that are prescribed can be modified if needed.

Role of the Recovery Coach

A newer concept in addiction recovery treatment is one that that I think holds as much or even more potential than any traditional treatment. This is the role of the Recovery Coach.

So just what is a Recovery Coach? First, I'd like to share with you what a Recovery Coach is *not*. A Recovery Coach is not an AA or NA sponsor and is not a counselor. A Recovery Coach is unlikely to give you advice on what your next move in life should be or tell you how you can get and stay clean. A Recovery Coach is also not affiliated with any treatment program or any 12-step fellowship.

Instead, a Recovery Coach is a person you work with personally who *will allow you to figure out what the best and honest approach to recovery is for you*. First, you have to be willing to accept the idea that there may be someone who is objective and who is not going to judge your ideas. So long as you are being open, this person can guide you while you figure out the best moves for yourself in recovery.

A Recovery Coach will help you find ways to improve your situation—no matter how difficult it might seem—through a combination of motivational support, referrals, and planning. So though a Recovery Coach does not offer treatment, this person will help you to help yourself by making suggestions for the creation of a plan of action to avoid relapse, while building a strong support network in the recovery process.

In this way, the Recovery Coach ties into your own self-directed will to change for the better. With a Recovery Coach, you are the only one considered to be the expert in your own life. No one can make a more informed decision about what is best for you besides you. A Recovery Coach will present several available options along the way (and make suggestions). If you like to have options, then this approach could work well for you. After you work through the different possible avenues you could go down, the Recovery Coach will hold you accountable for your choices and decisions. The overall purpose of this relationship is to guide you to finding your own path to wellness and recovery.

There has been a lot of recent interest in the Recovery Coach and also sober companions who help to positively monitor and encourage the lifestyle adjustments that ultimately lead to long-term recovery. The Recovery Coach should not be confused with a program sponsor. A sponsor helps you achieve an understanding of the 12 steps of AA or NA. A Recovery Coach helps you achieve an understanding of your motivation, choices, and, ultimately, your life. One does not replace the other. You could have both a sponsor and also a Recovery Coach if that is what you choose.

My own purpose as a certified health coach is to support people in achieving and maintaining a solid foundation in recovery by first understanding each client's personal circumstances. I work with clients who are motivated to make changes that will lead to better relationships, careers, and happiness. I can do this by e-mail, phone, or in-person, depending on what my clients feel is best for them and also what is realistic in terms of location and schedule.

Remember that any personal life coach, health coach, or recovery coach will challenge you, while also supporting you to make better choices. If you want someone in your life that genuinely wants to help you with what is most important to you today—whether that is finding resources and support for addictions, finding a job, finding a home, reducing your stress, or taking charge of your mental and spiritual well-being, a Recovery Coach may be the answer.

6

Nourishing Your Authentic Self

AS YOU CONNECT more with your recovery network, your personal commitment to recovery and overall wellness will begin to emerge. This happens because you are taking control of all the factors that influence your wellness. You are depending on your own choices to create the life you want.

When you can listen to and respond to your body's messages, you are in a powerful position. This is because you are the one who is in the driver's seat of your life now. Step-by-step, each positive change that you make brings you closer to a clean and sober lifestyle.

After everything that's been covered here so far, would you believe that working your recovery program and a wellness lifestyle go hand in hand? If you are ready for the self-destructive behaviors of addiction to be replaced with repair, restoration, and renewal of your mind, body, and spirit, then read on.

You are not responsible for your disease of addiction, but *you are absolutely responsible for your recovery*. You can begin today by taking your own health inventory and defining where you believe you are. What are your current goals for your health? How good is your overall health today?

First, think about what things in life are truly important to you and some potential goals that you would like to reach. All of these things are actually tied into your overall mental and physical health.

Goals can be short-term. Staying sober for today. Organizing your room. Making a new friend. Finding a good meeting location. Goals can also be longer-term. Would you like to find a career? Go back to school? Would you like to have a family someday? Would you like to repair your relationships? What will it take to reach these goals? And what do you think might have prevented you from getting closer to these goals in the past? If you have continually gotten in your own way, you can change that. Do not get overwhelmed.

Regarding your health, would you say there is a lot of room for improvement? Also think about the immediate health benefits that you would like as soon possible. These could include anything from increased energy to stress reduction or even an overall peaceful state of mind. What do you want? It's okay to want things. Recognizing your goals and your needs is a first step towards getting to where you want to be in your life. It can be done one step at a time.

What you eat has a lot to do with how you feel. In fact, what you eat can be extremely related to your mood and your emotions on a daily basis. Substances have taken a toll on your body. You know that physically this makes you very unhealthy. Chances are you have some nutritional deficiencies. They can show up as negative feelings, depression, anxiety, and irritability, all of which can severely interfere with your ability to recover well.

With this information, as well as what is known about supplemental nutrients, you can begin to make decisions about what you eat that are so important to your recovery. You can take steps to create an overall balanced diet plan knowing that your brain's ideal function is tied into the balance in your body and brain.

There are four essential neurotransmitters that are responsible for the balance of your energy and mood. These include serotonin, catecholamines, GABA, and endorphins, and each may have a distinctly dramatic effect on your mood, depending largely on their availability in your body (Ross 10). A brain that is deficient in one or more of these chemicals, through drug abuse and poor diet, can produce negative moods.

Here's an example: Serotonin is a natural antidepressant, so if you are low in this naturally occurring biochemical, you are going to feel negative, worried, and irritable. On the other hand, if you are balanced in serotonin, you will instead be positive, confident, and happy.

GABA is a naturally occurring relaxation chemical. If you don't have enough of it you can feel stressed and overwhelmed. Likewise, if you have enough GABA your stress melts away.

With the right amount of endorphins, you will feel comfortable in your own skin and be able to experience pleasure more easily. But without enough endorphins you can feel downright miserable—ready to cry for no reason.

Catecholamines keep you energized, and without enough you are probably lacking in energy and feel lethargic throughout your day.

So what good is all this self-nourishment and brain chemical talk? The ultimate goal is for your body to heal itself. And it's a miracle that given half a chance, the body will heal itself, all by itself. You give it the right tools, and it's a super computer that can repair the cell damage, realign your brain chemistry, and get back to your whole health and wellness that was originally yours to begin with.

Have you ever seen a plant grow towards the sun? It's the same idea with the healing of the human body. The plant naturally gravitates toward the sun to be able to generate energy for itself through photosynthesis. This happens without any special attention to the plant, and it is able to sustain its own life. Whether young or mature, plants will bend towards the light during growth, naturally finding a way to thrive.

The human mind and body are the same way. You are the same way. Just as the plant needs healthy soil, air, water, and light to grown, the body needs a decent environment to start with. Once you give your body and mind the right environment and self-nourishment, you will find remarkable things begin to happen. The body, like the plant, will naturally heal itself and grow. And, as the body naturally heals, the brain and spirit tend to join along.

I am not going to cover the best diet for your healing mind and body in this book, since every person is individual, and diet should be tailored specifically to you and your health needs.

However, I urge you to speak to your healthcare provider about a healthy diet soon and get referrals to work one on one with a health coach to help make changes in dietary lifestyle that can quickly help you feel better. You have more control of this than you think.

You can also begin looking at ways that you can begin taking charge of your emotions through the food that you eat. To help you do this on your own, I have provided a short list of resources for eating in recovery in the back of this book. These resources introduce the power of nutrition and can help you create a master plan for a healthy recovery. Please take a look at this list of options in the resources list.

• • •

Becoming fully aware of yourself and addiction requires a certain type of mindfulness and honesty about the actions that led to today. On the road to recovery, you need to have a deep commitment to not going down the same path continuously. The best way to do this is to have a clear set of intentions. Just start with one. If you had to decide, would you want to avoid pain only for today? Or would you prefer long-term peace of mind and freedom?

Your vow to yourself to continually work toward recovery becomes a simple and rational decision that you make. You promise it to yourself in the morning, throughout the day, and before you go to sleep. The commitment is simple, but it takes stamina and perseverance. You will be continuously tested by the circumstances of your life, which is why your promise to yourself is so important.

Embarking on a long-term path to recovery is full of awesome rewards. The reward is not for your friends, family, or any significant other. The reward is for you. When you know that you have conquered the most difficult darkest hours, you will experience a joy and serenity in sobriety that you have never known before.

Part of your commitment will mean planning each of your days. Avoid persons, places, and things that are reminders or triggers. Dodge them at all costs. Replace the old life with your newly found environment, decisions, and people.

Living Well With Gratitude

A psychologist named Martin Seligman wrote about the benefits of a positive mindset coupled with gratitude on people's overall happiness levels. He recommends certain activities for boosting your gratitude level. One of his ideas is to write down three good things that happened to you today. Then continue doing this each day. You could think of this as a gratitude journal, and incorporate it into your daily recovery. Even if you do not actually write it down, be sure to proclaim it to yourself each day.

The reasoning behind this is that we tend to think too much about went wrong every day instead of what went right. This isn't to say that we shouldn't learn from the mistakes we made. But instead of always preparing for disasters, it's time instead to focus on the positives.

At the end of the day, think of just three things that went well. They could be anything. Ask yourself what made you happy about each. The idea is that by getting into the habit of thinking positively each day, you can actually change your outlook. It might feel strange at first, but give it a try (Seligman 2011, ch.2).

Part of being your Authentic Self is also committing to understanding your "signature strengths" (Seligman 2002, 263). In other words, think of all of your positive qualities, and list the ways that you use them in your life today. Then make a list of additional ways that you can take your strengths to another level. Identifying your positive qualities is another way that you can create authentic happiness from within. Recognize that everything that you need to be fulfilled lies within you if you simply take the time to find it.

Avoiding Self-Sabotage

My belief is that self-sabotage is nothing more than fear masked as avoidance, delay, and lack of self-awareness. You may fear failure. You may be afraid of ridicule. Maybe you think that you aren't going to please someone or that you are going to be judged. And, because of these fears, rather than try out some new behaviors and see if that works, you actually do things to sabotage what might be your best efforts. In this way, you'll never know if things would have worked out the way you wanted them to. You are also protecting yourself when you sabotage, since you never really fail anything if you don't put all your gusto into trying in the first place.

It's an interesting phenomenon. Maybe you have unrealistically high expectations of yourself and think that you need to do something perfectly if you are going to do it at all? This will, of course, prevent you from doing pretty much anything, because no one does anything perfectly. A little fear can actually be healthy.

If you are not in chronic addiction, some anxiety is good. Why? It can motivate you to complete something well. But in the middle of addiction fear has nowhere to go. It constantly plagues your thoughts and prevents you from taking any real positive action at all. This could be because of the result of past trauma or failure, or it could simply be part of a repeated acceptance of circumstances that you felt were totally beyond your control. The key is that feelings aren't fact.

Trust me. Nothing is beyond your control. You have as much ability as anyone else to imagine whatever it is you want to be or become. And you have as much capability to follow through and be whatever it is you want to be. You might find this hard to believe, but it is absolutely true.

I was taught this over the years by some unsuspecting people. In fact, my own self-sabotage didn't become obvious to me until someone pointed out to me that I could pretty much do anything that I wanted—that I was no less valued or worthwhile than the next person.

I probably didn't believe it at first. You might not either. You might have to find your fans and people to stand behind you, including a sponsor, therapist, or home group. But get your team on your side. You must believe that you have the innate ability to do whatever it is that you dream of doing. There is no reason that anyone else is more qualified than you.

Love Yourself First

Relationships with significant others are outside the scope of this book, but I did want to mention a small (but important) point about relationships related to early recovery. You might have already heard that romantic relationships are not recommended in the first year of being clean and sober. If you are beyond that first year, congratulations! If you are not, please know that the one and only most important person to focus on this year is beautiful you (and you alone). The main reason for this is that you must be number one to yourself before you can usually achieve a sustainable relationship.

Sure, it's possible you'll find yourself attracted to other people now. It's fine to feel that way, and even great to have lighthearted relationships. But complicated romantic relationships can take away from the time for discovering your path to recovery, as well as keep you from learning what can keep you on that path long-term.

It takes commitment, thought, and daily work to learn all you can about recovery. It also takes the same type of commitment and dedication for a romantic relationship to be successful. Before committing to a romantic relationship, my strong suggestion is to commit to yourself completely and fully for at least a year. Once you have gotten clear on your own intentions and goals, as well as the personal recovery process that works best for you, you will be in a better place to begin any serious relationship.

7

Relapse Ahead? Take a Detour Back to Yourself

A COMMON IDEA in recovery is that the craving brain remains a part of the person who has successfully stopped using. You probably know what I mean. One day at a time, one moment at a time even, a person can be consumed by the need to 'abstain.' This isn't a way to live long-term. Not only do you not need to live this way, you can easily be on the road to this changing. It's possible that even now a stray thought is enough to make one have a craving—a fight with a friend, a conflict at work, a flat tire.

The idea of a trigger is that there are persons, places, and things, which can inevitably lead back to an urge to drink or drug. The interesting thing though is that with addiction, just about *anything* could be a trigger. The list could be really long. Even things that you would normally think of as positive (if they are at all stressful in the particular moment) could become potential triggers.

In addition to persons, places, and things that were related to using, it's a good practice to recognize all types of triggers that are specific to you. What triggers you might not trigger another person. If you recognize your triggers ahead of time, you can learn how to manage and avoid situations and create strategies for avoidance in advance of the situation. An object, like drug paraphernalia, a song that reminds you of using, or even a strong emotion, can all be triggers. Since you need to get rid of triggers, you need to be especially attentive to this process.

Cravings are what then follow triggers—when you have the physical urge or compulsion to use. The body and mind are accustomed to feeling those euphoric feelings with drugs. How do triggers turn into physical cravings? This happens through an important process that embeds the memories that actually cause craving.

It begins when the neurotransmitter, dopamine, is activated, and the brain's hippocampus creates memories of the drug event. The part of the brain known as the limbic system is in control of the emotions of the brain and records the feelings that are tied to the event. When using alcohol or drugs, the hippocampus is switched on, and memories of the experience are recorded, including all the people, places, and things associated with the event.

At the same time, the limbic system creates a strong emotional response related to the event. So when you are no longer using and happen to come across these same people, places, things, sights and sounds related to the time when you were using, the hippocampus activates the dopamine system sending a signal that falsely tells you that you are about to experience a good feeling!

The thoughts get triggered and the strong emotional response comes along with it. This is, of course, putting the matter all really simply. But what you can take away from this is that your cravings are somewhat conditioned in your brain—in the same way that Pavlov's dog was conditioned to respond by salivating when a bell was rung—thinking that it was about to get a treat.

What is critical is that you recognize all of your triggers. If you do, this response can be undone in the same way that it was created. Understanding how it works helps, too.

How can you begin? Make a complete list of places, people, times, and activities that contributed to drug use or that you find associated with them. Next, make a list of the places, people, times, activities that are not associated with use. It is important to identify as specifically as possible all the situations that may create triggers for you. And to completely avoid them. You can also identify your zones of safety.

It's not uncommon to relapse in addiction. It can be extremely frustrating, but it is not a sign of failure. It is simply another opportunity to succeed once that relapse has happened. This isn't to say that you should accept that a relapse is going to happen. It does not need to. It is definitely preventable, and if you continue creating a strong program, you have a great chance of avoiding it. But don't feel that if a relapse happens, you should give up.

On the contrary, take what you've learned, and "deconstruct" your relapse. What I mean is, analyze it. See how it happened, and take the steps to not let the same thing happen again.

Have you ever lost something and then had to retrace your steps? If you can go back in time and visit each place that you were in your mind, you can often find what you've lost. This concept is similar.

Go back in time and retrace what led to the relapse. What you lost is obviously your sobriety/yourself. But you can find yourself again. Do this together with your sponsor, Recovery Coach, or counselor. Discover where the mistake in judgment was made. Was it a person that you could have avoided? Were you lonely? Were you irritable? Is there any way that the situation could have been prevented with a little planning? Could you have reached out to someone when you had a trigger? Did you react to a negative situation hastily? What actions could you have taken instead?

Remember that you can and always should feel your feelings. It's what you do with the feelings and the actions that you take that keep you on your recovery path. You can avoid making that mistake again. You just have to decide to.

Smells, sounds, people, and even your dreams can remind you of a time when you were active in addiction. Keeping them top of mind and talking about how to minimize and avoid triggers is important.

Stress and anxiety can also be important causes of relapse. When you are stressed and anxious, you are impulsive and your decision-making can be poor. Not all stress can be avoided. But you can eliminate or reduce stress each day. Learning relaxation techniques such as simple meditation and trying to keep your stress level low are important. You can also work with your counselor and/or Recovery Coach to help you learn new ways to help decrease stress and anxiety.

Another surprising road to relapse is celebrations. These are events where you might have used before, so they can provoke triggers and imagery that can lead to alcohol or drug use quickly. Only you know when it is safe for you to attend these types of events. Tread carefully, and never take the gift of sobriety for granted.

Simply Tools for Conquering Cravings

Sustained recovery is a daily challenge. When you encounter a trigger—that is, a person, place, or thing, that creates a craving, there is a complex mechanism going on. Despite the fact that you know there are very negative consequences, your triggers are giving your brain the message that a strong reward is about to come. This overpowers your logical motivation to avoid drugs and alcohol.

The vulnerability to relapse is real. And managing the powerful impulses requires work. The best tools you have are greater self-understanding and awareness. You create them. There are a few really good places to start.

One tool that you can always turn to is known as the 5 'Ds' of addiction recovery:

Distract, delay, distance, determine, and decide

I'm sure you've heard that it's important to control your urges and impulses for sustained recovery. As in…if only you could control yourself, then you wouldn't have a problem. It's sad that the disease of addiction is so poorly understood. There is so much that goes into triggers, cravings, and the overall process that leads to relapse.

You know how complicated it is, and you know that you wish you had complete control of it. Yes, it's true that there is an impulse control issue that is going on. But that is really oversimplifying it. Your brain is craving because of a complex set of neurochemical processes that has been created over a long period of time. For now, it is enough to have a few tools in your back pocket to use whenever you need them. Remember, you can always take what you like, and leave the rest. That is, use whatever tools work for you. The Five D's include:

Distract-Change your surroundings and pick up an activity to immediately get away from the situation that is triggering your craving or urge.

Delay-Take your time and breathe deeply. Don't make any immediate decision. Be sure to slow down however you can. If you get a craving, delay for five minutes while easing into another mindset as your craving subsides.

Distance-Place a good physical distance between you and the offending substance, person, place, or thing that is triggering your emotional response or craving.

Determine-Determining is what you do right before you make your final decision. This is a place to pause and carefully look around before your next move.

Decide-You are the one who knows what's right and what you need to do to get your mindset in a better place. You are the only one who can make the decision for you today.

The responsibility is yours. Slow down and think, own it, and then decide.

Start from the beginning repeating step one (distract) and continue through these steps as needed. Now that you are becoming your Authentic Self, you are empowered to "polarize" opinions and ideas (that is, to look at all sides of the situation), organize your thoughts, and make decisions that feel good to you.

Distraction ideas:
- Take a walk through a park or down the street
- Ride a bike around town
- Take out some favorite old pictures to look at
- Go to a movie you've really wanted to see
- Light some candles and relax
- Call a friend—one who you trust and you know cares
- If you have one, play with a pet
- If you don't have a pet, go get one—any pet you can manage
- Take a nap
- Take a shower
- Play a musical instrument
- Write in a journal
- Go shopping
- Exercise – it releases stress and makes you feel better quickly
- Make a delicious snack
- Go to an enlightening meeting
- Have a cup of coffee or tea

- Read a good book
- Meditate and breathe
- Play a game

• • •

The acronym "H.A.L.T." is also an old standby and widely mentioned in recovery. It stands for "Hungry, Angry, Lonely, or Tired." Any one or a combination of these situations can lead to a dangerous emotional mindset that may have you falling back into old beliefs and patterns. The H.A.L.T. acronym may have been originally started in a 12-step program, but it is now common knowledge in recovery programs.

H.A.L.T. is useful for just about anyone who wants to keep a "pulse check" on their emotions. Just ask yourself if you are feeling any one of these four things at any given time of day. Here is a little more about each to help you get the most out of this easy self-care tool

Hungry
The 'H' stands for hunger. Hunger may be simple hunger for food, which, of course, can leave you irritable. But too much hunger for food alone can also leave you susceptible to hunger for food of a different sort—that is hunger to have your emotional needs filled. In order to be of sound mind, you need to first nurture your body. By not getting too hungry, you can be assured that your blood sugar is stable, your thinking is clear, and you are not mistaking agitation, emotional needs, and even cravings for what is nothing more than a need for a sandwich.

Angry
The 'A' stands for angry. There is absolutely nothing wrong with anger as an emotion. It's natural to feel angry sometimes. However, is it possible that rather than expressing anger in a healthy way, you have used drugs or alcohol to mask that anger in the past? If this is the case, you may not be used to feeling your anger fully. If this sounds like you, it may feel terrible to get angry while in a sober state. Your anger can also come out masked as self-destruction, criticism, and resentment towards others.

It's important that you learn to share your anger in constructive ways and determine its cause, or else it will not be productive. It will be destructive. You can do this through an honest, calm approach to what is upsetting you. You cannot control others' reactions to your feelings. But you can control yourself.

For the time being, realize that anger can be associated with fear, feelings of powerlessness, or even hurt. It's important to get together with a professional who is skilled in coaching on these issues so that when you do have natural anger, it is expressed in a constructive, healthy way.

Lonely
The 'L' is the next part of the H.A.L.T. acronym and is most obviously dangerous. My closest friend, Christina, used to get extremely lonely. No one who was close to her really knew quite how lonely she felt. She didn't seem lonely at all. She even had a smile on her face almost every day. It would have been important for her to reach out when she felt lonely to people that she could trust.

Isolation is a coping mechanism that is used to avoid pain and repress emotion. When you feel lonely, please reach out to someone that you can trust—even if this isn't what you usually do—so that you do not ever become too lonely. Address the cause of any tendencies that you have to isolate. Work on continually finding and building friendship and community in local recovery groups. They are often right around the corner.

Tired
The 'T' in H.A.L.T. stands for tired. Why is being tired a danger? Well, it's not if you are on your way to bed, and if you are getting enough rest each night. The danger is in exhaustion and not treating your body with enough rest and relaxation. At this point in your recovery, you need to practice extreme self-care. This means ensuring you are not physically and mentally tired. When we are not getting enough rest, this can turn the most common everyday situation into something completely overwhelming. This is the last thing you need. And it can be easily prevented with a good night's sleep. If you are having trouble sleeping, please seek the care of a healthcare and/or wellness professional.

Persons, Places, and Things

Do not interact with people who use. This, of course, goes without saying, and is an obvious rule. You'd think it wouldn't even have to be said. Yet it really can't be broken. I've actually seen this over and over again—where a person in recovery thinks an exception can be made—where someone with a good amount of clean time didn't think that they would be susceptible to slipping up. It was somehow necessary to be with someone or go someplace that was definitely a "danger zone."

You can be sure that this is practically *never* a good idea. No matter how well-intentioned you are. No matter how much you want to see that friend, or how much you think a person needs your company, or how much you miss someone who is in active addiction. Addiction is crafty. Addiction is deceiving. It will grab you when you least expect it. Think of it as any disease in remission that you wouldn't want to be re-exposed to. You know that you cannot be in certain places and with certain people, and, quite simply, there can be no exceptions—particularly in early recovery.

Stay away from neighborhoods where you used. Locate new places to spend your time. New restaurants. New activities, and new spots to enjoy life. Create original experiences in locations you've never seen. If you usually drove a certain way to get to work or to a friend's house, try a different route. Change everything up as completely as possible. Making things as fresh as you can is a great overall strategy. Stay away from people and places that upset you or fill you with a sense of dread. If you are at a point in your life where being around alcohol will be a trigger, then do not go to that party, place, or event. It's that simple. The more you practice this, the more your brain will eventually be reconditioned. Less triggers=less craving. Avoid the triggers. Banish the craving. Time heals.

Continually resist the urge with the proper tools and support. Your body will heal and eventually no longer come to associate those triggering people, places, and things with euphoric emotions. Eventually triggers will fail to produce cravings, and they will become fewer and farther between. But you must be diligent about it. Abstinence of triggers (and substances, of course) is the surest way to banish your cravings.

When you do come across a trigger and cravings become uncontrollable, turn to your sponsor, use H.A.L.T. and remember the five D's (as discussed in previous paragraphs).

Other strategies include:

Talking it out. Don't hesitate to call a friend, a sponsor, a trusted person, and tell them how you feel. Get yourself to a meeting as soon as you can. There's almost always one the same day. Whoever it is that you are speaking with must be a person that 'validates' your feelings. When you are with someone that validates your feelings, you are sure that they understand, or that they want to understand. This person is patient, and also willing to help you distract yourself. Be as honest and open as you feel comfortable with being. The more open and honest, the better off you usually are in recovery.

Know that cravings do not last forever. They are self-limiting. Through distraction, you will find that your cravings will diminish. From going for a walk to going to the movies, simply pick up and find something to occupy yourself.

Keep a clear head. Realize that resisting your craving puts you one step closer to not having that urge. A clear head also lets you realize that conquering the craving will have positive outcomes, including a continued path to sobriety. Make a list of all the positive results of the moves you are now making. For example, if you conquer the craving today, you will be able to show up for work, feel proud of yourself, be a better friend, and be that much closer to ridding yourself of cravings. On the other hand, think of the consequences of not conquering a craving: Loss of your job, loss of a friend, loss of your health, serious relapse, and all the difficulty that comes with it.

Stress management techniques are also important since *cravings are natural and will subside.* Remember, you may not be able to eliminate one-hundred percent of your triggers, but you are the only person who has control over your thoughts. Be patient and definitely reward yourself for not giving into the temptations. Stress reduction can help tremendously. Be sure to ask your therapist and/or healthcare provider about stress management options. Be open to learning about these techniques, including yoga, massage, meditation, acupuncture, and speaking with a person trained as a Recovery Coach.

Mediation is especially useful in early recovery. It can lower your anxiety, your heart rate, and give you a feeling of well-being. Time spent in active addiction is time that you are not connected to your emotions and your body. You can leave your daily routine anytime, any day by taking a few minutes to slow down and purposely breathe in a way that will calm and renew you. Try a simple meditation for 2 minutes per day:

- Find a quiet place to sit and relax without distractions
- Inhale deeply through your nose. Imagine that you are inhaling light, peace, and love
- Exhale slowly through your mouth. Imagine exhaling fear and anxiety
- Focus your attention on your breathing
- If your mind wanders, simply bring your attention back to your breathing

Conquer your craving One of the most positive ways to conquer a craving is creating a positive space in your mind. Close your eyes and imagine a sober time in a place you enjoyed with favorite people. Try anti-craving behavioral strategies such as a 5-minute contract in which you decide to not act on the desire to use for only 5 minutes at a time.

Instead of focusing on the craving, during that 5-minute time period, create extremely distracting activities for yourself. The craving will get weaker, and you will learn through repeated success of this method that you are more in control of this than you once thought—that you can, in fact, ride this wave. A trained counselor will be able to help you cope and create new behavioral strategies for getting through early cravings.

Remember that having a craving is normal and that you are not doomed to relapse. Try to learn all that you can about your cravings and your triggers so that you can manage them.

There are also a handful of non-addicting medications that you can review with your healthcare provider to determine if this course of treatment could be useful to reduce your cravings. Be open with your healthcare providers and counselors, and remember that you are responsible for your own body and mind. You will get the most out of your relationship with your healthcare provider if you are open and honest. If you do not feel heard, keep searching until you find a professional that you feel you can trust and are comfortable with.

A Word on Co-Occurring Disorders

As mentioned in an earlier chapter, co-occurring disorders, such as anxiety, depression, bipolar disorder, and ADHD can all impact people who are in recovery if they are not properly managed in conjunction with the addiction itself. Substance use can go hand-in-hand with co-occurring disorders. Sometimes it's hard to say which came first…the substance use or the co-occurring disorder. Some people believe that a mental health condition can cause substance abuse, and others believe that the substance use causes the mental health disorder. I personally think that it could be a bit of both in most cases.

Either way, the two often co-exist, and treating one without the other can lead to repeated relapse, since there is a condition there that is going left unchecked. Stress, trauma, abuse, learning disabilities, depression, as well as a number of other disorders, can all co-occur with substance abuse.

It is thought that many people who become addicted to drugs or alcohol are "self-medicating" for an underlying mental health-related condition. Without seeking help for that problem, relapse is likely to occur. Be sure that whatever program or treatment you choose is best for you and your individual situation. Your total assessment should include a wide range of possible causes. Both the addiction and the underlying cause(s) need to be addressed simultaneously.

8

Your Dreams and Beyond:

Your Safe, Sober, and Spiritual Self

THERE IS A lot of wisdom in the idea that small changes yield big results. This concept is a little difficult to take literally and can be challenging to follow through on. It requires patience (which you may need to purposely work on). Today, the most important thing to be aware of is this "small change focus" —at least at the beginning of recovery, where all change needs to be around little differences each day.

If you are focusing on the long-term results only, instead of the small steps needed each day, then change cannot happen. Why? You cannot get to any goal without the steps in between. Therefore, try to think simply and focus on day-by-day changes. One small step at a time actually gets you up the mountain. And if you take these small steps, you'll achieve much more than you thought possible. Each day of your purposeful focus will eventually add up to the long-term results you are looking for.

What doesn't work is the silver bullet approach. Any magical quick fix is not sustainable. There is no such thing as an instant solution. Anything worthwhile requires continuous and purposeful action one day at a time. So stick to your small goals and observe what happens. Jack Dickson said, *"If you focus on results, you'll never change; if you focus on change, you'll get results."*

• • •

Little behaviors and positive new habits lead to greater self-esteem, mood enhancement, new positive relationships, creativity, more energy, and increased freedom. With the intention to change, you can create new levels of consciousness about what you want today and what you want long-term. You can begin to see the creations that result from the very first baby steps. And like a baby, if you fall you get back up.

You may be beginning to feel more peace with yourself as you veer away from the need for immediate gratification. When you realize that becoming truly and authentically free from substances requires courageous daily acts, you begin to earn the rewards of recovery.

Your intermediate goals could be anything from building new friendships to going back to school to learning anything new. Whatever you decide your goals are, know that you can arrive at them from sticking to just that one small step a day. If you are already at that first goal, then examine how far you have come and be sure to keep track of your accomplishments, even if they seem minor to you. You should never short-change yourself. Give yourself credit whenever you deserve it. And as you learn from past mistakes, also take inventory of what you have been doing right each day. Meditate on it.

You can measure your success by careful self-reflection. How are your energy levels? Are you sleeping better? Are you making new connections? Are you enjoying activities that you didn't before? Whatever your intermediate goals, look back on where you came from and check in with yourself daily. Being aware of where you were and where you are going keeps you from coming to a halt and getting stuck.

And if you should hit a roadblock, do not become discouraged. You can get right back on track. When you practice being aware, you can recognize this sooner rather than later. Check in with a friend or sponsor frequently, so that you have a double check on yourself.

Your success will not happen immediately but comes on gradually in stages. Each day you may be a little better than the day before. Sometimes you may take one step forward and two steps back. The important thing is that you keep going forward. With that kind of determination, you will see the results add up.

What can you do to become more ready for longer-term goals? Begin by reciting them out loud and writing them down. You've taken all the small steps, and now your decisions are becoming a little more complex. There is more to sort through. Make a few bigger decisions, and take a look at your situation immediately after each event. These decisions could include anything from how much you exercise each day to deciding which strategies you will use to help you control stress. How did this work out for you?

If you are conscious of this process, you will see that continually checking in and choosing what works for you will bring you gratification today. Self-awareness will also help you continue to lead a good life in the days, months, and even years ahead.

• • •

We live one day at a time, and this is a popular approach to sobriety. Yet we need something to live for. We need love, passion, and creative outlets. We need relationships, satisfying jobs or careers, financial security, good health, a social life, and spirituality. As you begin to create your Authentic Self by tapping into your natural Wild Card, you will begin to discover new things about yourself that you never knew.

It's possible that you aren't exactly where you want to be yet. That's okay. You will get there. As you tap further into your Authentic Self, you begin to realize what areas of your life are out of alignment—whether it be your social life, your creativity, or your job, and tune into the next step to take to move forward in these areas. Decide how you could create some accountability. Write it down. Talk it over with someone.

A Health Coach is a great person to help hold you accountable to your short- and long-term goals. A Health Coach can also help you recognize areas where you can connect to your highest values and follow your heart as you continue to progress in recovery.

By creating and showing up each day, you have moved forward—one baby step at a time. Each challenge you have faced has helped you get a little clearer on where you have come from and where you are going.

Working through your fear is an important part of the process of growth. Don't let fear be a roadblock in your recovery. Just recognize it as a natural human emotion. Accept your fear and make that fear work for you by letting it guide you to the best action that's right for you today.

For example, in the past, you may have been looking for happiness in the wrong places. Having an optimistic perspective is what is important. We are conditioned to survive and push through natural fear. You can't avoid it. You wouldn't be human if you could avoid fear. Taking courageous actions *regardless of the fear* will bring you to your longer-term goals and, ultimately, to a self-loving feeling that is key to lasting and empowering recovery.

According to Tal Ben-Shahar, the secrets of happiness lie in having a purposeful and meaningful life. What does this mean? In this type of scenario, personal fulfillment is the meaning of happiness. This would include, for example, a job that meant more to you than just a simple paycheck. It would include working at something that is, of course, paying you fairly, but also feels enriching and important to you as a person.

If you want to get up each day to do the job just because it brings you happiness, you might be onto something. It could be that being a parent might be fulfilling to you. Or maybe being a good friend. Whatever it is that brings you serenity and satisfaction is tapping into something bigger than material gain or the immediate gratification that you were used to.

Another way of looking at this would be defining your choices and actions as ones that create both current and future happiness. Pleasure in the here and now (the present) is important, but long-lasting happiness stems from participating in activities in life that also fulfill a purpose—that benefit you or someone else in the future.

In other words, you can be doing something that brings you joy in the moment. That's a great thing. We have to enjoy life for sure. But if you aren't also building towards something bigger for the future, then it will not lead to ultimate happiness tomorrow. You could apply this principle to relationships in your life, to school, your job, or to a potential career.

You could even apply it to the food that you eat each day! We can break this down using what Tal Ben-Shahar calls the "Four Hamburger Theory" (Ben-Shahar, ch.2). Let's suppose that you are going out to your favorite restaurant and you are about to order a hamburger. The idea is that you can choose one of four hamburgers that are on the menu. Here's the catch: The hamburgers are really a comparison to the choices you make in life. Each hamburger represents a different type of choice that you can make each day. Remember, there are four hamburgers that you can choose from.

The first hamburger is delicious, but it isn't good for you. Therefore, it has a present benefit (that is, it tastes great right now) but it doesn't have a future benefit (because it's completely unhealthy). The person who chooses this hamburger has the mindset of the pleasure-seeker. The person who lives solely in the moment. This person lives as though the only things that matter are today's fun and pleasure.

The second hamburger doesn't taste quite as good (maybe it's a vegan burger), but it is *good for you*. So this second hamburger doesn't have a present benefit (maybe you don't even like it). But it does have a future benefit because it is healthy and full of nutrients. The person who chooses this hamburger has the "rat race" mindset. The person who participates in the human rat race thinks, "If I suffer enough today—work hard enough and sacrifice for everyone—then tomorrow I will get my reward." Unfortunately, this rarely works because, of course, the rat racer isn't enjoying life in the present at all. And who knows—he may never get to.

The third hamburger does not taste good, and it isn't good for you either. So there is really no reason to order this hamburger at all. It's tastes terrible, and it's made of junk. The person who chooses this hamburger has the mindset of the nihilist or the rebel. This is the person who has turned his or her back on happiness completely. This person lives in despair and is so disillusioned from past experiences that he or she thinks there is no longer a point to anything. I personally would not choose this hamburger.

Now the last or fourth hamburger on the menu is *the perfect hamburger*. Why? The fourth hamburger has both an immediate benefit (in that it is juicy, tastes fantastic, and has special sauce). But it is not just a delicious burger. It also has a future benefit since it is made with a higher-quality meat that is especially nutritious.

This isn't really about the actual hamburger but what it symbolizes. What does this fourth hamburger represent? How can you apply the 'hamburger theory' to your life? This fourth hamburger is really meant to illustrate, not just the best food choice to order off a diner menu (one that tastes good and also happens to be lower fat or organic), but really the best type of *choice* that you can make on any given day in your life—be it in your relationships, your career, and, yes, even your food.

If you make any decision that has an immediate benefit to you and that also fulfills something for your future benefit, then you can enjoy today's pleasures and also be on the way to your ultimate destination. The fourth hamburger represents a realistic mindset which accepts that if we set ourselves up to be happy purposefully by making good choices, we will have a greater chance of that happiness both today and in the future. There is no reason why you, too, can't create that lasting happiness.

By choosing the fourth hamburger (remember this is a just an analogy), you are living happily in the moment, one day at a time, but you are also living in a way and making choices that can help deliver on your dreams and goals.

Once you have discovered what it is that is bigger than yourself—that is, what your future benefit might be, then you can really begin to achieve your longer-term goals.

So how do you figure out what your longer-term goals are? So that you can choose hamburger number four? You can't choose the best until you know what the best is for you. The answer lies in becoming the best version of yourself that you can possibly be. The highest version of yourself is grateful, moves forward, and believes in something bigger than immediate self-gratification. Challenges that you experience in life will help you become clearer about what your special strengths are. What your Wild Card is. Your success will not happen overnight. New challenges help you become more clear about who you are, and each day you will discover more than the day before.

As human beings, we all have the ability to overcome adversity. Remember that we are all like plants that grow towards the sun. We don't naturally give into adversity or bad weather. When you run into bad weather, take out your umbrella, stand firm, and find new ways to let the roots grab hold. The sun will come out soon.

Healing Your Authentic Self

I want to help you be powerfully aware that you can achieve greatness during recovery by tapping into your Authentic Self. It has been my goal to help you begin to set intentions for yourself. Remember to be patient and know that gradually, step-by-step, one day at a time, you can achieve a state of recovery that feels, not simply 'clean,' but also healing.

You have probably heard that addiction is not just a state of being physically addicted to a drug, but that total recovery is dependent on your state of mind. You can heal with adjustments in attitudes, beliefs, environment, diet, sleep, and spiritual relations—all leading to the discovery of your Authentic Self, your purposes, and your dreams. Most diseases (and addiction is no different) are caused by imbalances of the body-mind continuum. By taking a closer look at the root causes of addiction; fixing what you can control day by day; and taking extremely good care of yourself, you can begin to find the beauty within your spirit and soul.

Remember that we are all individuals, and your personal customized program is at the core of your recovery. Only you can take responsibility for your own self-made program. It's hard to take responsibility for your program at all if it isn't yours alone. Remember that no matter what any particular recovery program or book talks about, you can create your own recovery process. This happens in a way that you manufactured so that it has individual purpose and meaning. It is up to no one else. You will gain great satisfaction by knowing that you are in recovery—not alone—but in a way that is completely yours to be proud of.

• • •

From here on out, please be careful. We cannot always be perfect, but we should try to make decisions that put us in the best possible place in recovery. Choose the safe route if you are unsure, and don't be afraid to reach out to friends, family, your Recovery Coach, sponsor, or counselor when you are at a crossroad, feel stuck, or think your situation is too risky to your mental health and/or physical well-being.

Above all else, stay sober. Obviously, progress and self-creation gets challenging if sobriety is not practiced one day at a time. Of course, there is much more to sobriety than simply not having a substance in the body. Staying sober is a complete set of attitudes that you can gain from self-learning, AA or NA meetings, individual or group counseling, medication assistance, nutrition, stress reduction techniques, recovery coaching, sponsorship, and any combination of these customized for yourself by yourself.

And remember that a program of recovery is a program of spirituality. You will hear this often wherever you go in the world of recovery. What you might not hear is that the core of being spiritual is being present in the moment. Your spirituality is also something created by you—not imparted on you by someone or some group. Spirituality that is forced isn't necessarily spiritual at all. By spiritual, I mean getting in touch with your inner core, the innocent state of existence that was you when you were born.

Every infant is born in a divine state, unaffected by any negative experience or messages. Babies are born playful, ready to trust, and perfectly innocent—to experience love and happiness. You were, too. Over time, the baby is conditioned to competition with the human race—to believe that he/she is not good enough, not smart enough, and not attractive enough.

We are taught that there is never enough time, never enough money, never enough love. Over time, instead of growth into something more mature, we sometimes go backwards and are conditioned to forget who we are.

But there is no reason that you cannot re-achieve what was your birthright and remember the qualities that made you happy, authentic, and human. You can make a choice to nurture yourself and remember that you can create whatever happiness you want.

First, value your body by giving it the best self-care you can. By doing so, you become available to what the world has to offer you each day. Self-care is a discipline, so it may not come automatically. But self-care equals self-love. Loving yourself by starting with daily acts of self-care will impact how you show up every day in the world.

Next, believe that everything is happening now exactly how it is supposed to! Believe that your life is unfolding perfectly. Believe that life has your back. When things go wrong (and they will) you can then be open to the next opportunity without any regret and without fear and anxiety or of the unknown. Trust that the right people will show up in your life exactly when they are supposed to. Your job is to be open to realizing this, and recognizing this divine opportunity when it happens.

Part of this belief is also deciding what it is that you want. You may not know exactly where you want to be yet, but you may have an idea. Visualize it in your mind's eye as clearly as you can. Do this frequently. Ask yourself how you would show up each day in the world if you already had everything that you needed. How would you approach people? How would you deal with negativity from others? You would probably be more at ease. You might splurge on gifts for yourself. You would probably throw away things you no longer needed and get rid of negative influences in your life.

Try to live this way anyway. Live as if you have everything that you need. Keep your heart open. Trust that the universe has something to offer you that is bigger than yourself, and continue to visualize your success—whatever that might mean to you. Remember that the reason you may have not lived this way is that you have been conditioned to a lot of very negative beliefs about what the world has to offer you. Reject these beliefs.

Another key to being in touch with what the world has to offer is to give generously. Give exactly the same thing that you want to receive. You may have heard, "What goes around comes around." Set down your troubles, and practice generosity. Then see what happens in return. The universe is full of possibilities and may have an interesting way of responding.

• • •

As you continue in your own healing, you can begin to stand confidently in the truth of who you are and to share that with others. In order to do this you need to tell your story and at the same time give it up—be willing to release it. What does this mean? In order to achieve complete freedom, you need to realize that your past story does not need to define your present moment. In order to continue creating your Authentic Self, you will need to be in the now—not the past—to move forward. Tell your story, release your story, and live in the present.

Know that though the past has been traumatic or less than you would have dreamed, it does not need to represent your present. They no longer need to be connected to each other. There should be no place that you've ever been or any experience so horrific that you are stopped from living in a way that is beneficial to yourself.

Forgiveness is a powerful tool. Sometimes it is hard to forgive others, but I encourage you, to the greatest extent possible, to at the very least forgive yourself. Once you move out of your own self-blame and blaming others, you become open to trust. If you do not do this, then your mind may unconsciously search for people and situations that you cannot trust. By forgiving yourself, you are trusting yourself, too, to make the right types of decisions now. You are letting go of the perception that you are not lovable.

Finally, reclaim who you really are and why you are here. Let go of the notion that there is a person or situation that can take that away from you. It is simply not true, no matter what your past experience has shown you. The present is new. Never give your power away to anyone ever again.

Now is the time for radical authenticity beginning with extreme self-love. Remember that your story is okay to learn from, but it is not okay to continue living in. Accept that sometimes you will need to surrender to whatever circumstances come your way. But the one thing that you can always practice is self-care, no matter what life brings. Continue loving yourself through both the calms and the storms. Love yourself until you feel your heart and hear your mind telling you what your next step is. Through learning self-love you will eventually be able to look over your shoulder to the past. And you will know that learning to be in the present and loving yourself unconditionally is all that was needed.

The disease of addiction tells the story of your life. That is okay, too. Accept it lovingly. Share your story with those you trust. Listen to your own story, and learn from it. Be with your truth completely. Then let go of it. Feel your feelings soberly. Embrace yourself and heal today, and a little bit more each day. And when you are ready, recreate the authentic you. I wish you all the happiness in the world—the joys that you were entitled to from the day you were born.

Resources for Recovery

Recovery Support Groups

Alcoholics Anonymous (AA)
212-870-3400
www.aa.org

Narcotics Anonymous (NA)
Nonprofit alcohol and drug abuse fellowship
818-773-9999
www.na.org

SMART Recovery
Self-management and recovery training
www.smartrecovery.org
866-9515357 or 440-951-5357

Friends and Family Support Groups

Nar-Anon Family Groups
12-step program for families and friends of addicts
www.nar-anon.org

Families Anonymous
12-step fellowship for family and friends of addicts and alcoholics
800-736-9805
www.familiesanonymous.org

Al-Anon/Alateen
12-step program for families and friends of alcoholics
888-4AL-ANON or 757-563-1600
www.al-anon.alateen.org

General Information on Drug and Alcohol Abuse

National Institute on Alcohol Abuse and Alcoholism
301-443-3860
www.niaaa.nih.gov

National Institute on Drug Abuse
301-443-1124
www.nida.nih.gov

Substance Abuse and Mental Health Services Administration
800-662-HELP
www.samhsa.gov

Private Organizations

Faces and Voices of Recovery
202-737-0690
www.facesandvoicesofrecovery.org

Hazleden Foundation
800-257-7810 or 651-213-4200
www.hazleden.org

Finding Addiction Treatment

Substance Abuse Treatment Facility Locator
www.findtreatment.samhsa.gov

National Association of Addiction Treatment Providers
717-392-8480
www.naatp.org

The Fix
Featured news and resources for early addiction recovery
www.thefix.com

Buprenorphine Physician and Treatment Locater
www.buprenorphine.samhsa.gov/bwns_locator

National Alliance for Medication Assisted Recovery
methadone.org

Treatment Match.org
www.treatmentmatch.org

AIDS/HIV Treatment and Support

AIDSInfo
Information on HIV/AIDS Treatment and Prevention
www.aidsinfo.nih.gov
1-800-HIV-0440 (1-800-448-0440)
TTY: 1-888-480-3739
Outside U.S.: 1-301-315-2816
Hours: Monday through Friday 12:00 pm to 5:00 pm (Eastern Time)
E-mail: ContactUs@aidsinfo.nih.gov

International HIV/AIDS Alliance
www.aidsalliance.org

AVERT
www.avert.org

Eating for Recovery: Recommended Reading

Beasley, Joseph D., and Susan Knightly. *Food for Recovery: The Complete Nutritional Companion for Recovering from Alcoholism, Drug Addiction, and Eating Disorders.* New York: Crown Trade Paperbacks, 1994.

Bitman, Mark. *How to Cook Everything.* New York: Macmillian, 1998.

Larson, Joan Mathews. *Seven Weeks to Sobriety: The Proven Program to Fight Alcoholism through Nutrition.* New York: Ballantine, 1994.

Ross, Julia. *The Mood Cure: The 4-step Program to Take Charge of Your Emotions-today.* New York: Penguin, 2004.

Siple, Molly. *Eating for Recovery: The Essential Nutrition Plan to Reverse the Physical Damage of Alcoholism.* Cambridge, MA: Da Capo/Lifelong, 2008.

Selected Bibliography

Ameisen, Olivier. *The End of My Addiction.* New York: Sarah Crichton, Farrar, Straus and Giroux, 2009.

Beasley, Joseph D., and Susan Knightly. *Food for Recovery: The Complete Nutritional Companion for Recovering from Alcoholism, Drug Addiction, and Eating Disorders.* New York: Crown Trade Paperbacks, 1994.

Beckman, Chris. *Clean: A New Generation in Recovery Speaks out.* Center City, MN: Hazelden, 2005.

Bennett, Sam. *Get It Done: From Procrastination to Creative Genius in 15 Minutes a Day.* Novato: New World Library, 2014.

Ben-Shahar, Tal. *Happier: Learn the Secrets to Daily Joy and Lasting Fulfillment.* New York: McGraw-Hill, 2007.

Esko, Edward. *Yin Yang Primer: A Guide to the Unifying Principle of Macrobiotics.* Becket, MA: One Peaceful World, 2000.

Foote, Jeffrey, Carrie Wilkens, Nicole Kosanke, and Stephanie Higgs. *Beyond Addiction: How Science and Kindness Help People Change.* New York: Scribner, a Division of Simon & Schuster, 2014.

Gammill, Joani. *Painkillers, Heroin, and the Road to Sanity: Real Solutions for Long-term Recovery from Opiate Addiction.* N.p.: Hazleden, 2014.

Hoffman, John. *Addiction: Why Can't They Just Stop?* New York: Rodale, 2007.

Jay, Debra. *No More Letting Go: The Spirituality of Taking Action against Alcoholism and Drug Addiction.* New York: Bantam, 2006.

Jay, Jeff, and Debra Jay. *Love First: A New Approach to Intervention for Alcoholism and Drug Addiction.* Center City, MN: Hazelden Information & Educational Services, 2000.

Klosterman, Lorrie. *Drug Dependence to Treatment.* New York: Marshall Cavendish Benchmark, 2008.

Kuo, Tsun-Chen, and Feng-Ming Ho. "The Role of Acute Stress in the Enhancement of Immunity Mechanism by Acupuncture." *Merit Research Journal of Medicine and Medical Sciences* 1.4 (2013): 047-48.

Larson, Joan Mathews. *Seven Weeks to Sobriety: The Proven Program to Fight Alcoholism through Nutrition.* New York: Ballantine, 1994.

Levine, Noah. *Refuge Recovery: A Buddhist Path to Recovering from Addiction.* New York: HarperCollins, 2014.

Lin, Jaung-Geng, Yuan-Yu Chan, and Yi-Hung Chen. "Acupuncture for the Treatment of Opiate Addiction." *Evidence-Based Complementary and Alternative Medicine* 2012 (2012): 1-10.

Lombard, Jay, Christian Renna, and Armin A. Brott. *Balance Your Brain, Balance Your Life: 28 Days to Feeling Better than You Ever Have.* Hoboken, NJ: John Wiley, 2004.

Newport, John. *The Wellness-recovery Connection: Charting Your Pathway to Optimal Health While Recovering from Alcoholism and Drug Addiction*. Deerfield Beach, FL: Health Communications, 2004.

Ratey, John J., and Eric Hagerman. *Spark: The Revolutionary New Science of Exercise and the Brain*. New York: Little, Brown, 2008.

Rosenthal, Joshua. *Integrative Nutrition: Feed Your Hunger for Health and Happiness*. New York, NY: Integrative Nutrition Pub., 2008.

Ross, Julia. *The Mood Cure*. New York: Penguin, 2002.

Ruden, Ronald A., and Marcia Byalick. *The Craving Brain: The Biobalance Approach to Controlling Addictions*. New York: HarperCollins, 1997.

Rundio, Al, and Stephen D. Krau. *Nursing and Addictions*. Philadelphia: Elsevier, 2013.

Sandor, Richard S. *Thinking Simply about Addiction: A Handbook for Recovery*. New York: Jeremy P. Tarcher/Penguin, 2009.

Seligman, Martin E. P. *Authentic Happiness: Using the New Positive Psychology to Realize Your Potential for Lasting Fulfillment*. New York: Free, 2002.

Seligman, Martin E. P. *Flourish: A Visionary New Understanding of Happiness and Well-being*. New York: Free, 2011.

Siple, Molly. *Eating for Recovery: The Essential Nutrition Plan to Reverse the Physical Damage of Alcoholism*. Cambridge, MA: Da Capo/Lifelong, 2008.

Snelling, John. *The Buddhist Handbook: A Complete Guide to Buddhist Schools, Teaching, Practice, and History*. Rochester, VT: Inner Traditions, 1991.

Urschel, Harold. *Healing the Addicted Brain: The Revolutionary, Science-based Alcoholism and Addiction Recovery Program.* Naperville, IL: Source, 2009.

Wilkinson, Jonathan, MB ChB MRCP FRCA, and Richard Faleiro, BSc (Hons) DCH FRCA. "Acupuncture in Pain Management." *Continuing Education in Anaesthesia, Critical Care & Pain* 7.4 (2007): 135-38

Share Your Recovery Journey

I HOPE THAT you have been inspired to begin creating your Authentic Self in recovery with some of the guidelines I've shared. Feel free to reach out to me anytime. I'd be interested in hearing about your progress! I would also be happy to work with you privately to help you reach your recovery goals.

I have begun writing another book focusing on your firsthand accounts of recovery, the milestones you've reached, and how you've integrated your Authentic Self into a program of recovery.

It's important to realize that setbacks will be encountered along the way. It's in the way that these are managed by you that is really interesting, as well as how your obstacles are overcome. Whatever setbacks or successes you have had, I'd love to hear from you. I am hoping to weave in these circumstances as well as speak directly to family members and friends in my upcoming book.

Please contact me anytime at lisa-michele-wilson.com or lisamichele@comcast.net.

About the Author

Lisa Michele Wilson is a medical writer and Certified Health Coach, having received her coaching education from the Institute for Integrative Nutrition in New York City. Ms. Wilson specializes in the area of wellness and recovery by providing emotional support, education, and inspiration to those aiming for long-term recovery, as well as assistance to families dealing with the disease of addiction. She is dedicated to moving people to action and empowering those in recovery, their families, and friends through her insight and experiences.

Lisa Michele speaks on addiction and recovery in the central New Jersey and New York metropolitan area. For more information on coaching and wellness in recovery, visit Whole Health + Wellness at www.lisa-michele-wilson.com. For media or speaking inquiries, please email lisamichele@comcast.net.

www.ingramcontent.com/pod-product-compliance
Lightning Source LLC
Chambersburg PA
CBHW022118040426
42450CB00006B/754